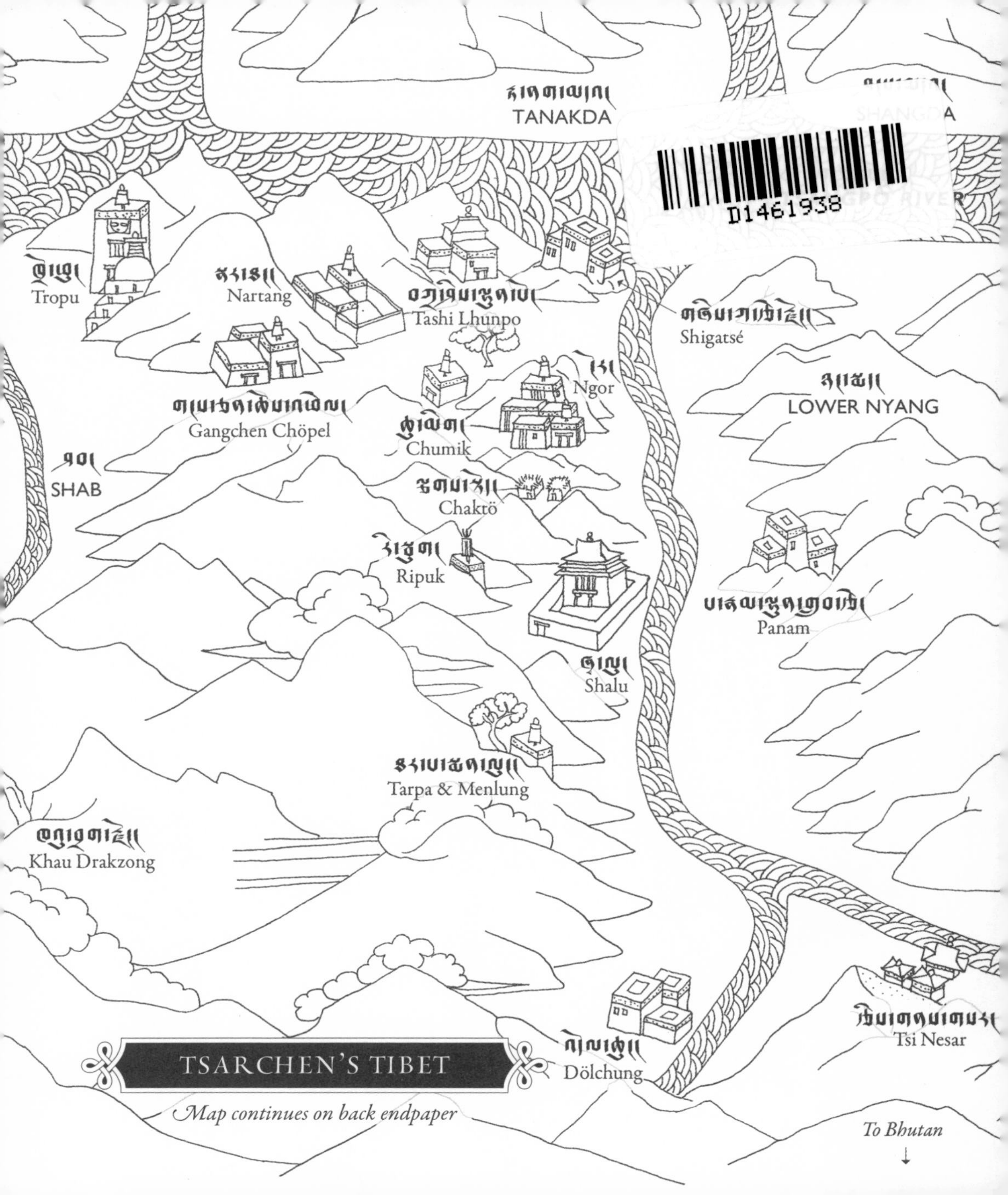
TANAKDA
Tropu
Nartang
Tashi Lhunpo
Shigatsé
Ngor
LOWER NYANG
Gangchen Chöpel
Chumik
SHAB
Chaktö
Ripuk
Panam
Shalu
Tarpa & Menlung
Khau Drakzong
Tsi Nesar
Dölchung
TSARCHEN'S TIBET
Map continues on back endpaper
To Bhutan
D1461938

Song of the Road

TSADRA FOUNDATION is a U.S.-based nonprofit organization that contributes to the ongoing development of wisdom and compassion in Western minds by advancing the combined study and practice of Tibetan Buddhism.

Taking its inspiration from the nineteenth-century nonsectarian Tibetan scholar and meditation master Jamgön Kongtrul Lodrö Tayé, Tsadra Foundation is named after his hermitage in eastern Tibet, Tsadra Rinchen Drak. The foundation's various program areas reflect his values of excellence in both scholarship and contemplative practice, and the recognition of their mutual complementarity.

Tsadra Foundation envisions a flourishing community of Western contemplatives and scholar-practitioners who are fully trained in the traditions of Tibetan Buddhism. It is our conviction that, grounded in wisdom and compassion, these individuals will actively enrich the world through their openness and excellence.

We are delighted to ally with Wisdom Publications in making this volume available in the English language.

Song of the Road

THE POETIC TRAVEL JOURNAL OF TSARCHEN LOSAL GYATSO

Cyrus Stearns

Wisdom Publications • Boston
with Tsadra Foundation

Wisdom Publications, Inc.
199 Elm Street
Somerville MA 02144 USA
wisdompubs.org

© 2012 Tsadra Foundation
All rights reserved.

No part of this book may be reproduced in any form or by any means, electronic or mechanical, including photography, recording, or by any information storage and retrieval system or technologies now known or later developed, without permission in writing from the publisher.

Library of Congress Cataloging-in-Publication Data
Blo-gsal-rgya-mtsho, Tshar-chen, 1502–1566 or 7.
Song of the road : the poetic travel journal of Tsarchen Losal Gyatso / Cyrus Stearns.
pages cm
Includes bibliographical references and index.
ISBN 1-61429-055-5 (cloth : alk. paper)
1. Blo-gsal-rgya-mtsho, Tshar-chen, 1502–1566 or 7—Travel. 2. Sa-skya-pa lamas—Biography. I. Stearns, Cyrus, 1949– II. Blo-gsal-rgya-mtsho, Tshar-chen, 1502–1566 or 7. Rtogs brjod lam glu dpyid kyi rgyal mo'i dga' ston. III. Blo-gsal-rgya-mtsho, Tshar-chen, 1502–1566 or 7. Rtogs brjod lam glu dpyid kyi rgyal mo'i dga' ston. English. IV. Title.
BQ942.L644A3 2013
294.3'923092—dc23
[B]
2012037698

ISBN 9781614290551; eBook ISBN 9781614290667

17 16 15 14 13
5 4 3 2 1

Cover illustrations: Sixteenth-century painting of Tsarchen Losal Gyatso by the madman Chökyi Dorjé (Smyon pa Chos kyi rdo rje). Photograph courtesy of Sakya Dolma Phodrang. According to the inscription, this portrait shows what Tsarchen actually looked like when meditating on the Dharma protector Caturmukha. Background photograph of Gyantsé, Tibet, by Andrew Quintman. Map courtesy of Pimpin de Azevedo. Cover and interior design by Gopa & Ted2, Inc. Set in Garamond Premier Pro 11.375/16.95.

Printed in the United States of America.

This book was produced with environmental mindfulness. We have elected to print this title on 30% PCW recycled paper. As a result, we have saved the following resources: 10 trees, 4 million BTUs of energy, 815 lbs. of greenhouse gases, 4,422 gallons of water, and 296 lbs. of solid waste. For more information, please visit our website, www.wisdompubs.org.

CONTENTS

Illustrations · vii

Preface · xiii

Introduction · 1

Notes to the Introduction · 17

Map of Tsarchen's Tibet · 22

Celebration of the Cuckoo:

MY AUTOBIOGRAPHICAL SONG OF THE ROAD

by Tsarchen Losal Gyatso · 25

Notes to the Translation · 124

Bibliography · 157

Index · 163

ILLUSTRATIONS

1. Tsarchen Losal Gyatso. Clay portrait crafted during Tsarchen's lifetime and preserved in his monstery of Tupten Gepel. Photograph by Matthew Akester. xviii

2. Kunpang Doringpa. Woodcut of Lord Doringpa as he appeared to Tsarchen in a vision. After Ngawang Losang Gyatso, *Sunlight of the Doctrine of the Explication for Disciples*, 401. 2

3. Khau Drakzong. Ruins of Lord Doringpa's hermitage. Photograph by Cyrus Stearns. 3

4. Tupten Gepel Monastery. Tsarchen's monastery in the upper Mangkar Valley. Photograph by Matthew Akester. 5

5. The Great Stūpa of Jonang. Completed by Dölpopa Sherab Gyaltsen in 1333. Photograph by Michael Sheehy. 7

6. Bodong. Photograph by Matthew Akester. 8

7. Geding. Photograph by Matthew Akester. 10

8. The Great Stūpa of Gyantsé. Photograph by Cyrus Stearns. 12

9. Pema Wangchen Yangsang Tröpa. Detail of a painted maṇḍala. After Ngor Thartse Khenpo Sonam Gyatso 1983, 1: Image 133. 42

10. Tropu. The ruins of the great stūpa completed by Tropu Lotsāwa in 1234 are visible in the left foreground. Photograph by Matthew Akester. 57

11. Nāro Khecarī. Detail of a painted maṇḍala. After Ngor Thartse Khenpo Sonam Gyatso 1983, 1: Image 69. 58

12. Chumik. Photograph by Matthew Akester. 68

13. Ngor Monastery. As it appeared before 1959. After *Chöyang* journal, 1991, 63. Photograph courtesy of David Jackson. 73

14. Shalu Monastery. Photograph by Matthew Akester. 74

15. Ripuk. Photograph by Thomas Wild, courtesy of Matthew Akester. 78

16. Panam Fortress. As it appeared before 1959. After Richardson 1998, plate 86 (between pp. 330 and 331). 84

17. Tsi Nesar. As it appeared before 1959. After Tucci 1973, illustration 60 (p. 81). 92

18. Yamdrok. Photograph by Matthew Akester. 100

19. The Dharma Protector Takshön. Painting published in Essen and Thingo 1989, 1: no. 133 (p. 215). 108

20. Rinpung Fortress. As it appeared before 1959. After Schäfer 1943. Photograph courtesy of Isrun Engelhardt and Matthew Akester. 122

The apparent images
of existence and peace
in this dream drama
are apparitions of one's
mind alone—nothing else.

The essence of mind itself
is beyond what is to be realized
and the act of realization.

The hair of the tortoise
covered the lotus of the sky.

The sound of the echo
called to the moon in water.

The horns of the rabbit
killed the son of the barren woman.

I tricked myself before
with pointless confusion.

Mind that can't be gazed upon—
I've gazed upon now.

The truth that can't be seen—
I've seen.

How to express what
can't be expressed in words?

Kye Ho!
Now practice is over.
Kye!

—Tsarchen Losal Gyatso

PREFACE

EVEN A SHORT BOOK can take a long time to write. Dezhung Rinpoché and Chogyé Trichen Rinpoché planted the seeds for this one in the form of stories they told me in the 1970s and 1980s about Tsarchen Losal Gyatso, a peerless tantric master of the Sakya tradition of Tibetan Buddhism. Several of the tales I first heard are translated in this book, including Tsarchen's dramatic encounter with the goddess Vajrayoginī in the form of a haunting, sick young woman.

Dezhung Rinpoché was the most gifted storyteller I have ever met. For about six years I knew of Tsarchen's life and teachings only from him. Then in 1979 I was able to borrow an old blockprint edition of the Fifth Dalai Lama's biography of Tsarchen that E. Gene Smith had obtained and loaned to David Jackson. Finally able to read the full story of Tsarchen's life, I became fascinated with his own account of a journey made in 1539. The Dalai Lama had inserted many passages from Tsarchen's travel journal into the biography, but it was not clear to me whether the entire journal or only certain parts had been included. In

1980 Dezhung Rinpoché said he had never seen the journal in his homeland, the eastern Tibetan region of Kham. And when he later visited Sakya Monastery in Tsang (west-central Tibet) and searched through the library of the Drölma Podrang, he did not find it there. It seemed to have survived only as a series of fragments in the biography.

In 1981 I moved to Bodhnath, Nepal, to continue learning from Dezhung Rinpoché and Chogyé Trichen Rinpoché. There I extracted all the journal quotations in the biography and wrote them in a small notebook. They seemed to fit back together in complete form (as the Fifth Dalai Lama did indicate), but I remained uncertain because of the abrupt end of the journal and the lack of a colophon. I continued to ask every Sakya master I met if they had seen the journal except as quoted in the biography. H. H. Sakya Trizin, Chogyé Trichen Rinpoché, and Khenpo Appey Rinpoché had also never seen the text as a separate work.

During the same year, I would often go and spend time with Chogyé Trichen Rinpoché (the head of Tsarchen's tradition) in his tiny dirt-floored room beside the huge stūpa of Bodhnath. Tsarchen's patron and disciple, Darpa Rinchen Palsang, had written a versified biographical supplication that the Fifth Dalai Lama had also inserted into his biography of Tsarchen, breaking up the verses and using them as a narrative thread around which he wove the broader fabric of the story. I wrote these verses out in sequence and put them back together to form the original text, which also did not exist independently. For several months Chogyé Rinpoché explained this work to me, sometimes consulting my photocopy of the biography, but most often just speaking his mind. I made a translation of the text and was also able to ask more questions about Tsarchen's travel journal and hear many stories about him. As these sessions continued, Rinpoché taught me a beautiful versified guruyoga focusing on Tsarchen, which Jamyang Khyentsé Wangpo is said to have written when inspired by the incredible clay portrait of Tsarchen at Tupten Gepel Monastery.

For the next twenty-five years I would sometimes pull out my old notebook and read through Tsarchen's memoir. I tried to translate the sections I had written out, but the difficulty of the language and the nagging uncertainty of whether the text was complete discouraged me. But in 2006 I decided that I should just prepare a translation of what I had. Within a month of that decision, I received a message from Matthew Akester in Nepal saying my old friend Guru Lama (who has published countless rare Sakya texts) had obtained a copy of an old manuscript of some of Tsarchen's writings that included the journal. Almost as if circumstances had flushed it out of hiding, a crucial manuscript had emerged at just the right moment.

Guru provided a photocopy of the original cursive manuscript and the new version he was preparing for publication. When I compared the complete manuscript to the individual sections I had copied in my notebook, they matched, with the exception of a few words and spelling differences. The Fifth Dalai Lama had indeed spliced Tsarchen's full journal into the biography. This also means the reading transmission for Tsarchen's work has remained unbroken to the present day.

Tsadra Foundation's president, Eric Colombel, and vice-president, Drupgyu Anthony Chapman, accepted my proposal for translating the travel journal, and it was added to my list of projects that Tsadra Foundation generously supports.

This book would never have seen the light of day if not for Eric's profound commitment to the publication of significant works from all the Buddhist traditions of Tibet.

I am very grateful to Khenpo Gyatso, the principal and abbot of Sakya College in Dehradun, India, who answered my endless questions about the journal with great insight and patience, and to his secretary, Tsering Dhondup, who skillfully handled all our email communication. Without their help I could never have completed this translation with any hope of accuracy. Lama Tenpa Gyaltsen later clarified a few points that remained obscure, and David Jackson's helpful suggestions at the last minute were indispensable. H. H. Sakya Trizin graciously allowed his extraordinary painting of Tsarchen by Chökyi Dorjé to be reproduced on the cover of this book. Patricia Donohue kindly made arrangements for me to receive a photograph of the painting. I also thank Andrew Quintman and Michael Sheehy for their photographs. Matthew Akester took an early interest in this project, sending me copies of Tibetan manuscripts and many photographs, and searched tirelessly for an artist to craft a special map. As a result, Pimpim de Azevedo's wonderful drawing of the Tibetan landscape greatly enhances the story of Tsarchen's travels. David Kittelstrom's superb editing immensely improved my original text, and Gopa & Ted2's impeccable design created magic throughout the book.

Chogyé Rinpoché had sometimes urged me to translate Tsarchen's biography. I have not accomplished that task, but at least I have now translated Tsarchen's travel journal, which is the heart of the biography. Needless to say, any mistakes that linger are due to my own lack of understanding.

Tsarchen's journal is sometimes strikingly similar to the famous *Narrow Road to the Interior* (*Oku no Hosomichi*) of the Japanese haiku master Matsuo Bashō (1644–94), which records a journey taken in 1689, exactly 150 years after Tsarchen's trip. As with Bashō's classic, Tsarchen's text is written in a mixture of luminous prose and verse, with an immense amount of hidden meaning. Extensive notes to the translation are essential. I think of them as the result of a literary archaeological exploration to reveal the layers of meaning beneath Tsarchen's words, placing them in the context of the spiritual topography of the land he travels, the centuries of history and legend permeating the places he visits, his experience of the trip. In such a poetic work, however, multiple endnote numbers throughout the translation would be an unfortunate intrusion. The notes at the end of this book are arranged in the sequence that names, places, and other topics occur in the translation and are identified by page number.

After the introduction, I urge you to first read the entire journal in a single sitting without looking at the notes. This will allow Tsarchen to cast his spell, and you will gain an immediate, fresh impression of his memoir. Part of the power of such a work is its brevity. This allows us to experience the force of its totality, which would be frustrated or negated by turning to endnotes, taking a break to check email, or speaking with a friend. Set aside an hour or two and see into Tsarchen's life through his own words.

Tsarchen Losal Gyatso

INTRODUCTION

As I hear the life stories
of the root and lineal masters,
may the hairs on my body
vibrate with faith and delight,
like a peacock hearing thunder
from the clouds, and may
the blessing enter my heart.
—Tsarchen Losal Gyatso[1]

UNBEARABLE PAIN first drove the young man to his future teacher. Tsarchen Losal Gyatso (1502–66) was about seventeen years old when he arrived at the feet of the great hermit Kunpang Doringpa,[2] seeking a cure for the inflammatory disease torturing his leg. Weird and wonderful dreams followed, in which emanations of the Dharma protectors indicated the disease would continue for a number of years and then vanish without a trace. Tsarchen returned to Tashi Lhunpo Monastery, where he had been studying. One morning, at the large well in the monastery courtyard, he met a woman with shimmering eyebrows and facial hair. "Lord Doringpa says come to Khau quickly," she said. "This is his gift." Passing to him a small manuscript wrapped in cloth, she vanished. The book was the esoteric instructions of the three forms of Khecarī, or Vajrayoginī.

Tsarchen soon received a sealed letter from Lord Doringpa: "It would be good for you to receive the ripening and liberating oral instructions of the Vajrayāna. Come here." Overcome with joy and devotion, he set off for the isolated hermitage of Khau Drakzong, not far from Sakya Monastery. When he told Doringpa what had happened at Tashi Lhunpo and showed him the manuscript, the master just laughed, exclaiming, "Oh, my! Khecarī went to fetch you. This book is her Dharma cycle. Take it to the bookstacks for now." Tsarchen went there and saw in the middle of the pile of books a gaping hole from which the manuscript had been removed. He slipped it into place and it fit perfectly. He was filled with inexpressible faith and wonder.[3]

Kunpang Doringpa

For the next six years Tsarchen stayed with Lord Doringpa at his cliffside retreat, receiving all the esoteric transmissions of the Sakya tradition and also the complete Shangpa Kagyü teachings (Doringpa had been a disciple of the great Shangpa adept Tangtong Gyalpo, 1361?–1485). Doringpa passed to him the entire Lamdré, or Path with the Result, the Thirteen Golden Dharmas of Sakya, the secret transmissions of the Dharma protectors, and other

Khau Drakzong

profound teachings. Much of the key instruction took place in private, when they went for walks or had tea together. In this way, Tsarchen became Doringpa's supreme Dharma heir and the master of what came to be known as the Lobshé, or Explication for Disciples. He writes in his travel journal: "After meeting the great venerable lord Doringpa and receiving this Precious Teaching, I've had a deeply rooted certainty, with no yearning or hunger for any other master and oral instruction for achieving enlightenment."

Not long after the death of Lord Doringpa in 1524, Tsarchen traveled to the region of Ü for the first time, serving as an attendant to the master of the Khön family of Sakya, Dakchen Ngagi Wangchuk (d. 1544). He stayed for about eight years and later visited again for roughly six months. During these and later years Tsarchen studied with more than sixty masters of all traditions. He practiced their teachings in long retreats in both Ü and Tsang, once remarking, "Basically, there are no mantras of the new and old traditions of secret mantra that I have not recited according to the specifics of propitiation. Of them, this *śāsana* mantra of the protector has the greatest power. As I repeat this, fire is actually blazing around my string of beads."[4] In 1534 he ascended the teaching throne of Tupten Gepel Monastery in upper Mangkar, the valley of his birth. There he taught, meditated in retreat, and composed some important works, including the biography of Lord Doringpa, after many ḍākinīs urged him to do so in a series of amazing dreams.

Then, in the late spring of 1539, Tsarchen set out with a small band of mendicant yogins on a third journey east into Ü. This time he would stay for nearly two years. In *Celebration of the Cuckoo* he writes, "And if I resorted to the nectar of being homeless myself, a great change would most likely occur in the essence of mind within."[5] This vivid travelogue or "song of the road" describes the first month or two of the trip, beginning from his hermitage of Tupten Gepel in Tsang and ending at Kyetsal Monastery on the southern border of Ü.[6] The Fifth Dalai Lama (1617–82) says Tsarchen's work is composed of "superb words and meaning, blazing with the light of majestic blessing," and asks, "Styled in finely alternating verse and prose, were Sarasvatī to have appeared in his throat and spoken, what more could she have said than that?"[7]

Tsarchen's journal covers only a brief period of his life, but the text and the trip are both of crucial importance. The small work is his largest autobiographical

Tupten Gepel Monastery

statement. Along with his collected songs or poems, it is the primary source for glimpsing who he really was, what he perceived and thought of the world around him, how he expressed his deepest feelings.[8] Tsarchen describes outer episodes, inner impressions, and secret visions. Since he wrote it himself, it is definitive. He did choose what to include and omit in the memoir, but there is little danger of fabrication or elaboration, unlike what can occur when another person writes a biography at a later time. This is why the journal and the experiences described in it are given such prominence in the earliest biographical supplication to Tsarchen, which his patron and disciple Darpa Rinchen Palsang composed in the sixteenth century, the extensive biography the Fifth Dalai Lama wrote in 1676, and the verse biography that Khyenrab Jampa Ngawang Lhundrup (1633–1703) composed.[9]

We do not know how or when Tsarchen composed his travel journal. Perhaps he based it on an informal diary kept during the trip. Perhaps he wrote only the beautiful text that has survived. But a year or so before he departed for Ü, Tsarchen spent time in retreat meditating on Sarasvatī, the goddess of the fine arts. During the retreat a rain of white flowers fell, he heard the sweet sound of Sarasvatī's lute, and finally saw her face and received her prophetic words. This caused an incredible gift of eloquence to blossom, and whatever he wrote naturally came forth as poetry.[10] Tsarchen's entire journal can be read as a mixture of prose poetry and verse poetry, impossible to fully convey in translation. As the celebrated poet W. S. Merwin has written, "I have tried to translate poetry (in full awareness of the limitations, the utter impossibility of the enterprise)."[11]

Celebration of the Cuckoo is not simply a travel journal. The richness of the language, imagery, and visionary experiences set it apart from other works of the same genre in Tibet.[12] Tsarchen's memoir is a treasure trove for people who are able to read carefully, recognize the allusive depth of the work, feel the resonance of the people and their stories, the places and their histories. The full range of his character is on display. He is not afraid of straight talk or revealing his feelings. Humor, love, and compassion coexist with caustic wit, irritation, and harsh criticism.

Tsarchen and his companions slowly pass through the countryside, crossing high passes and rivers, descending into deep valleys, visiting hermitages, estates, temples, villages. He rides on horseback because of his bad leg. His students walk on foot. Each person carries a small white tent to live in during the trip. Only thirty-eight years old at the time, Tsarchen is already a superb master of the tantric systems transmitted in the Sakya tradition and also of Nyingma, Shangpa, and Kagyü practices. During the trip he gives various Sakya and Nyingma initiations and transmissions. And his wish to meet other masters and receive teachings never ceases. Of the Sakya and Nyingma masters he visits, two are already his teachers; a few he has never met before. He writes brief yet memorable vignettes.

Traveling north from his home in the Mangkar region, one of Tsarchen's

The Great Stūpa of Jonang

first stops is the great hermitage of Jonang, where his group pitches their little tents near the huge stūpa that Dölpopa Sherab Gyaltsen (1292–1361) had completed in 1333. Tsarchen is filled with awe when he witnesses the strict meditation practice of the men and women, and vows to lead a similar life. At the nearby monastery of Chumolung, he visits his teacher Ratnabhadra, an eccentric master whose specialty is the Nyingma transmission of the Northern Treasures, specifically a certain form of the wrathful deity Hayagrīva that is already one of Tsarchen's favored practices. Ratnabhadra's odd behavior deeply impresses Tsarchen's monks.

Turning east, the group arrives at Bodong, where Tsarchen's old teacher

Bodong

Gorumpa Kunga Lekpa (1477–1544) has been invited to the palace of the ruler. Gorumpa is a fascinating figure. He had been the head of the Jonang tradition for twelve years, retiring from the throne in 1527, but he is an accomplished master of the Lamdré and other esoteric transmissions of the Sakya tradition. Tsarchen praises him as the greatest Sakya master of the time and emphasizes that Gorumpa has been his most important teacher in the years since the passing of Lord Doringpa. Visiting Ngakchang Kunga Rinchen (1517–84) at Geding, Tsarchen sheds tears of joy at the impressive abilities of the young throne holder of Sakya.

That same evening the group arrives at the temple and stūpa of Tropu. Here the tale shifts into another dimension when Tsarchen encounters a strange young woman crouched on the circumambulation path. His description of what happens next is the narrative heart of the journal. This episode and the one at Tashi Lhunpo (related at the beginning of the present introduction) are the two most famous events involving Vajrayoginī in the one-thousand-year history of the Sakya tradition.

In a humorous incident when camping beside an enchanting spirit-lake of the goddess Maksorma, Tsarchen is mistaken for the former ruler Silnönpa (now a monk) of the powerful Rinpung dynasty, a major political force in Tibet during this period. Crossing a high mountain pass the party arrives at the ancient temples of Chumik Ringmo, filled with special images. But Tsarchen is saddened to see the dilapidated condition of the place. At Ngor Monastery (an important center of the Sakya tradition) they pitch their tents in a pasture, and Tsarchen gives an initiation for the Dharma protector Mahākāla on a temple rooftop.

Geding

Back on the road, he stops to camp on the estate grounds of his paternal relatives (descendents of famous grand governors of Tibet) and unsuccessfully tries to remain unnoticed.

When the group reaches the monastery of Shalu, another mysterious woman appears and vanishes near Tsarchen. He visits special places there, gives and receives several initiations, and is offered some tea crucial for the trip, which brings him great joy. Sixteen years later he would become abbot of Shalu Monastery. Still farther to the east, when Tsarchen's monks go begging for alms at the Panam fortress of Lhundrup Tsé, the chieftain rudely snubs them. Using a cryptic traditional aphorism, Tsarchen expresses what he thinks of such worthless rulers.

At the next few stops along the way, Tsarchen receives teachings, a niece deceives him, and he offers initiations to a ruler. In the upper region of the Nyang Valley, his group visits Gyantsé, with its great stūpa and monasteries. They pitch their tents behind the fortress, but his companions end up sleeping in the mud when a rainstorm flattens them. Tsarchen wants to continue east from Gyantsé to Ralung Monastery and visit one of his teachers, Drukpa Ngawang Chögyal (1465–1540), the head of the Drukpa Kagyü tradition. But his hopes are dashed. The monks are in a rush, and his horse (which he describes as the substitute for his bad leg) is wearing out. They change their route and turn north, cross a soaring mountain pass, and come to Shambhar Monastery in Rong.

Rong is one of the ancient centers for the Nyingma practices of Takshön, the Dharma protector Mahākāla mounted on a tiger, who is the special guardian of Tsarchen's hereditary line. The master at Shambhar has actually beheld Takshön's terrible form. Before Tsarchen leaves, he too has been graced with chilling visions of the protector, omens that he will accomplish certain future deeds by means of this practice.

Crossing the Tsangpo River into the domain of the Rinpung dynasty in Ü,

The Great Stūpa of Gyantsé

Tsarchen immediately appreciates the benefits (as a poor traveler) of the strict laws of the local regime. This is highly ironic, because it is these very rules that will annoy him later. When he arrives at the large Sakya monastery of Kyetsal, his companions set up the tents in a nearby field; Tsarchen goes to the monastery, enjoys conversation with the master Dragkar Rabjampa (d. 1541?), and gives many tantric transmissions to the Kyetsal monks. He learns that the Rinpung ruler Ngawang Namgyal has extended an invitation to Karmapa Mikyö Dorjé, head of the Karma Kagyü tradition. The ruler has levied a mandatory tax on all his subjects to provide a lavish welcome for the Karmapa's visit. Everyone is excited but also in despair at the cost. The teachers and monks of Kyetsal Monastery have no choice in the matter because the Rinpung ruler is also their patron. Tsarchen finds the situation disturbing. He will not pay such a tax.

The uproar surrounding the state-sponsored spectacle of the Karmapa's famous encampment (composed of perhaps hundreds of large tents) does not impress Tsarchen, who is traveling with a band of itinerant yogins living in small tents. He does not meet the Karmapa but writes some harsh words about the scene and about Mikyö Dorjé, mostly critical of his involvement in political intrigues but also dismissive of his scholarship. Such comments are not unusual in Tibetan literature, where criticism between different masters and traditions (and sometimes even within the same tradition) is quite common. Tsarchen carefully emphasizes that he is critical only of certain activities of Karmapa Mikyö Dorjé. He stresses his sincere faith in the Karmapa and the Kagyü teachings, which he previously received from Karma Trinlepa (1456–1539), one of the Karmapa's main teachers. Though not mentioned, the Karmapa's vacillating hostility toward the Nyingma tradition may also have prompted Tsarchen's criticism.[13] The events at Kyetsal are the final episode in the travel journal.

After an absence of almost two years, Tsarchen returned to Tsang in early 1541. For at least the last part of his route, he retraced his steps, again meeting his teachers Gorumpa and Ratnabhadra at Bodong and Mount Lalung, and then continuing to the nearby hermitage of Jonang. Another of Lord Doringpa's main disciples, Jetsun Kunga Drölchok, was now the Jonang throne holder. Tsarchen did not send word that he was coming to visit, yet Kunga Drölchok knew without being told and had everyone go outside and line the main road in welcome. Other than the usual route, there was also a steep rock cliff that could only be climbed on foot. But Tsarchen rode a mule up the rocks. When people saw him approaching from the unexpected direction, they rushed over to offer greetings. It seems that the two masters were playing with each other—Kunga Drölchok preparing a welcome without being told of Tsarchen's visit and Tsarchen appearing from a different and seemingly impossible approach.[14] Tsarchen soon arrived back at his monastery of Tupten Gepel in the upper Mangkar Valley.

The last twenty-five years of Tsarchen's life were filled with dreams and visions of his teachers, past masters, and various deities. He spent time in retreat, visited other teachers, and transmitted again and again the most essential tantric systems of the Sakya tradition (and of the Nyingma and Shangpa) to the young masters who would become his principal Dharma heirs, especially Jamyang Khyentsé Wangchuk (1524–68) and Mangtö Ludrup Gyatso (1523–96). These two major disciples placed in writing for the first time the special instructions that Tsarchen had received from Doringpa and other masters, thereby preserving the previously oral tradition of the Explication for Disciples.

One morning in the early 1550s Tsarchen had a vision of three women carrying arrows adorned with silk. Descending from the sky on a long ladder, they said, "We have come to invite you." But he refused the invitation. He would not go because his parents were still living. The women climbed back up the ladder. Lord Doringpa had long ago warned Tsarchen that Vajrayoginī might soon take him to her paradise of Khecara and had advised him to practice techniques for extending his life for the benefit of the Buddhist doctrine.[15]

After dreams and visions of Lord Doringpa and the menacing protector goddess of Shalu, Tsarchen ascended the teaching throne of Butön Rinchen Drup (1290–1364) in 1555 and became the thirteenth abbot of Shalu Monastery. Four years later he retired to the region of his birth, the Mangkar Valley, and his disciple Jamyang Khyentsé Wangchuk took the Shalu throne.

In 1564, twenty-five years after the meeting with the Sakya throne holder Ngakchang Kunga Rinchen that Tsarchen describes in his travel journal, the rulers of the nearby regions of Dar and Donga went to war. The ruler of Dar, Rinchen Palsang, was Tsarchen's main patron, and two of Kunga Rinchen's wives were sisters of the ruler of Donga. The Donga army invaded Dar and destroyed the temple and images of the Dharma protectors at Tsarchen's birthplace of Mushong. The army returned the next year and surrounded the fortress of the ruler, where Tsarchen was staying at the time. According to the Fifth Dalai Lama's account, Tsarchen's ritual prowess finally drove them away.[16]

About two years later, one of Tsarchen's main disciples, Bökharwa Maitri Döndrup Gyaltsen (1514–75), came to make offerings and receive teachings. Some of Tsarchen's last words to him were: "I also have some enemies that must be subdued. But I'm old and that won't happen. So you disciples must subdue my enemies. The most potent enemies are the five poisons that cast us into saṃsāra. So these are to be subdued. Yet if the five poisons were utterly destroyed, there would be no causes for the five types of primordial awareness. That too won't happen."[17]

Soon after, in the fall of 1566, Lord Doringpa appeared in the luminous space of Tsarchen's meditative concentration. "Dharma lord, come up," he said, gesturing again and again. Tsarchen thus passed away into the purity of the basic space of phenomena, actualizing the thirteenth level of a vajra holder in the paradise of Khecara. From the luminous dark blue sky, filled with rainbows as though painted with a brush, a gentle rain of flowers fell, covering the earth with a wonderful, unknown fragrance. The Fifth Dalai Lama quotes the words of the Indian master Atiśa: "The skin of the snake is shed, but the snake dies not." For a person who has gained control of birth and death, passing away is nothing but an experience of moving from one residence to another.[18]

For many years after Tsarchen's death, his body of primordial awareness continued to appear to his different disciples (as had the Indian master Nāropa appeared to Lord Marpa Lotsāwa long before), teaching Dharma, giving prophecies, and offering encouragement. His precious physical remains were dressed in fine brocade robes, anointed with saffron, and placed in a jeweled casket full of salt. For the next fifteen years they received constant offerings, until they were finally enshrined in a gold and silver stūpa in 1581.

Tsarchen's legacy in the Sakya tradition today is profound. Most of the crucial Sakya tantric teachings (and all the special transmissions known as the Explication for Disciples) have been passed down through Tsarchen and his major Dharma heirs. His travel journal speaks across the centuries, living in its own continuous present, yet retaining the intractable strangeness of the past.

Notes to the Introduction

1. Tsarchen Losal Gyatso, *Supplication to the Masters of the Precious Teaching*, 243: *rtsa brgyud bla ma'i rnam thar thos pa'i mod/ sprin gyi rnga gsang thos pa'i rma bya ltar/ dad dang spro ba'i spu long cher g.yos te/ byin rlabs snying la 'jug par byin gyis rlobs.*

2. The Sakya master Kunsang Chökyi Nyima (Kun bzang chos kyi nyi ma, 1449–1524), the Hermit of Doring, was Tsarchen's main teacher. Usually known as Kunpang Doringpa (Kun spangs Rdo ring pa), he was the most important disciple of Dakchen Lodrö Gyaltsen (Bdag chen Blo gros rgyal mtshan, 1444–95), from whom he received the transmission of all the esoteric teachings of the Sakya tradition, especially those of the Lamdré and the Dharma protectors. For a brief sketch of Doringpa's life, see Stearns 2006, 255–56. For the definitive biography, see Tsarchen Losal Gyatso, *Marvels That Cause Body Hairs to Tremble with Faith*.

3. See Ngawang Losang Gyatso, *Sunlight of the Doctrine of the Explication for Disciples*, 464–67.

4. See Ngawang Losang Gyatso, *Sunlight of the Doctrine of the Explication for Disciples*, 497: *ngas gsang sngags gsar rnying gi sngags phal cher bsnyen tshad bzhin ma bzlas pa ye med/ de rnams kyi nang nas mgon po'i sngags shā sa na 'di nus pa che shos la 'dug ste/ 'di bgrangs pas 'phreng ba la dngos su me 'bar ba yong gin 'dug*. The protector is Mahākāla and the *śāsana* is his long mantra.

5. In the journal itself Tsarchen mentions the title as *Celebration of the Cuckoo: An Autobiographical Song of the Road* (*Rtogs brjod lam glu dpyid kyi rgyal mo'i dga' ston*). The Fifth Dalai Lama also uses the term *dga' ston* ("celebration") in the name. But the title page of the old manuscript contains the term *glu dbyangs* ("ballad") instead of *dga' ston*, even though *dga' ston* is found in the manuscript where Tsarchen names his work. And Tsarchen wrote at least three other texts with *dga' ston* in their titles. I have accepted the name Tsarchen uses within his work, which the Dalai Lama also gives in the biography. It is not so unusual for editors of Tibetan texts to use slightly different names on title pages and in colophons. The Tibetan text included in the present book is the reassembled sections of the travel journal quoted in Tsarchen's biography. See Ngawang Losang Gyatso, *Sunlight of the Doctrine of the Explication for Disciples* (Lhasa edition): 62a–64a, 64b–65a, 65a–65b, 66a–66b, 67a–67a, 67a–69a, 69a–69b, 70a–72a, 72b–73b, 73b–76a, 76a–78a. Every word of the Lhasa edition was compared to the same text in the Lamdré Lobshé (Lam 'bras slob bshad) collection and to the old manuscript and the recently

published edition of the travel journal. Some preferable words and spellings in the latter three versions have been adopted here, usually at the suggestion of Khenpo Gyatso.

6. Tsarchen specifically mentions that his trip began in the fifth month of the pig year (the summer of 1539). The last episode in the travel journal occurs when the Eighth Karmapa, Mikyö Dorjé (Mi bskyod rdo rje, 1507–54), has arrived in the Shu Valley (Gzhu lung pa). According to Pawo Tsuklak Trengwa, *Feast for Experts*, vol. 2: 1285, at the invitation of the Rinpung (Rin spungs) ruler Ngawang Namgyal (Ngag dbang rnam rgyal, b. 1494?), the Karmapa departed from his monastery of Tsurpu (Mtshur phu) in the first part of the fifth month of the pig year. Traveling by way of Üri (Dbu ri), he arrived in Shu. Therefore, Tsarchen's journal probably describes only about one, or possibly two, months of travel. For geographical information, see Ferrari 1958, 69, 161.

7. See Ngawang Losang Gyatso, *Sunlight of the Doctrine of the Explication for Disciples*, 520–21: *tshig don phun sum tshogs shing byin rlabs kyi gzi byin 'od du 'bar ba*, and 555: *bcad lhug spel legs nyams 'gyur dbyangs can ma/ mgrin par byon nas gsungs kyang de las ci*. Sarasvatī is the goddess of the fine arts, one of which is poetry.

8. Tsarchen wrote one other brief autobiographical sketch, an account of his mystical experiences involving a special form of Hayagrīva. See Tsarchen Losal Gyatso, *Sealed Secret Autobiography*. For his collected songs, see Tsarchen Losal Gyatso, *Radiant Light Illuminating the Fine Path*. I am preparing a translation of this collection.

9. See Darpa Rinchen Palsang, *Rippling Ocean of Blessed Nectar*; Ngawang Losang Gyatso, *Sunlight of the Doctrine of the Explication for Disciples*; and Khyenrab Jampa Ngawang Lhundrup, *Fine Vase of Blessed Nectar*. In Rinchen Palsang's work, nine of the fifty-one quatrains are devoted to the events of Tsarchen's brief journal. The Fifth Dalai Lama took Rinchen Palsang's verses as the basis for the extensive biography. It seems that he also incorporated all or parts of two other rare works, but both have now been lost: (1) the poet Darpa Sönam Lhundrup ('Dar pa Bsod nams lhun grub), nephew of Rinchen Palsang, wrote a commentary to his uncle's verses entitled *Moonlight of Elegant Explication* (*Legs bshad zla ba'i snang ba*), and (2) Jamyang Gawai Shenyen ('Jam dbyangs dga' ba'i bshes gnyen), abbot of the monasteries of Chökhor Yangtsé (Chos 'khor yang rtse) and Nyenyö Jashong (Mnyan yod bya gshong), wrote a biography based on the previous two texts entitled *Necklace of Marvelous Gems* (*Ngo mtshar nor bu'i mgul rgyan*). See Ngawang Losang Gyatso, *Sunlight of the Doctrine of the Explication for Disciples*, 634–36. In Khyenrab Jampa's text, three of the nine pages concern Tsarchen's journey, including several

of his songs (*mgur*) from the travel memoir. I am grateful to Dan Martin for telling me about Khyenrab Jampa's work and for putting me in touch with Vladimir Uspensky, who kindly sent me a photocopy of the text from St. Petersburg, Russia.

10. See Ngawang Losang Gyatso, *Sunlight of the Doctrine of the Explication for Disciples*, 512: *thugs rtsom gang mdzad snyan ngag tu 'gro ba'i blo gros kyi spobs pa nang nas rdol bar mngon*. The status of Tsarchen's poetic skill was emphasized to me in 1985 when Dezhung Rinpoché was about to compose the final verses of his biography of his master, Gatön Ngawang Lekpa Rinpoché (Sga ston Ngag dbang legs pa Rin po che, 1864–1941). Rinpoché asked me to bring him a volume of the Lamdré Lobshé collection from the University of Washington library so that he could read for inspiration Tsarchen's poetry at the end of his biographies of his master, Lord Doringpa, and Doringpa's master, Dakchen Lodrö Gyaltsen. Of special significance to Dezhung Rinpoché were the verses now placed as an epigram on page xi of this book. See Tsarchen Losal Gyatso, *Garland of Captivating Water Lilies*, 144: *srid zhi'i snang bsnyan rmi lam zlos gar 'di/ gzhan na ma mchis rang sems gcig pu'i 'phrul/ sems nyid ngo bo rtogs bya rtogs byed bral/ rus sbal spu yis nam mkha'i padma khebs/ chu nang zla ba brag ca'i sgra yis bos/ ri bong rwa yis mo gsham phrug gu bsad/ sngon chad don med 'khrul pas rang mgo bskor/ blta rgyu med pa'i sems la da ni blta/ mthong rgyu med pa'i don ni kho bos mthong/ brjod rgyu med pa tshig tu ci zhig brjod/ kye ho da ni nyams len zad do kye.*

11. Merwin 2008, 114.

12. Many old Tibetan travel journals (*lam yig*) are now available. Others are known only from titles mentioned in books. The work most similar to Tsarchen's text is certainly the journal of his teacher and friend, Jetsun Kunga Drölchok (Rje btsun Kun dga' grol mchog, 1507–66), another leading disciple of Kunpang Doringpa. Kunga Drölchok's journal describes a trip he took in the same general area in 1533, just six years before Tsarchen's journey. It seems likely that Tsarchen had read Kunga Drölchok's text and, since he visited Kunga Drölchok at Jonang near the end of his own journey, Kunga Drölchok could have read Tsarchen's work. Kunga Drölchok's memoir is also a mixture of prose and poetry, but with even more verse than prose. See Kunga Drölchok, *A Travel Journal to Dispel Darkness*. Other notable memoirs that have survived are the Sakya throne holder Gyagar Sherab Gyaltsen's (Rgya gar Shes rab rgyal mtshan, 1436–94) brief verse account of a trip to the eastern Tibetan region of Kham; an incomplete manuscript of Lhatong Lotsāwa's (Lha mthong Lo tsā ba, b. 1512) versified journal of a trip to Nepal; the Sixth Shamarpa, Mipam Chökyi Wangchuk's (Zhwa dmar Mi pham chos kyi dbang phyug, 1584–1630) prose and verse journal of a trip to Nepal; the prose and verse travel memoir of the

Tenth Karmapa, Chöying Dorjé (Karma pa Chos dbyings rdo rje, 1604–74), who was the Sixth Shamarpa's main disciple; and the verse account of the Nyingma master Rikzin Tsewang Norbu (Rig 'dzin Tshe dbang nor bu, 1698–1755). See also Newman 1996 for a discussion of some travel journals describing trips to the legendary land of Shambhala.

13. According to the Fifth Dalai Lama, Karmapa Mikyö Dorjé sometimes claimed that the secret mantra practice of the Nyingma tradition was "a perversion of Dharma" (*chos log*) but at other times observed the tenth-day celebrations of some later treasure discoveries of that tradition and showed devotion to implements of Vajrakīla practice. In a letter sent to the powerful ruler at Neudong, the Karmapa calls a certain Nyingma discoverer of treasure teachings "an emanation of Māra." This is like calling someone "a spawn of Satan." See Ngawang Losang Gyatso, *Sunlight of the Doctrine of the Explication for Disciples*, 554: *sne'u sdong gong ma chen por phul ba'i chab shog tu/ deng sang dbu ru byang phyogs brgyud 'di na/ gter stong lcang lo can zhes bdud sprul de.* The Karmapa also wrote a series of questions critical of the Nyingma tradition, which the Nyingma master Sokdokpa Lodrö Gyaltsen (Sog zlog pa Blo gros rgyal mtshan, 1552–1624) refuted in detail in 1576. See Lodrö Gyaltsen, *Dragon Roar of Scripture and Reasoning.* The letter the Fifth Dalai Lama quotes and the letter of critical questions aimed at the Nyingma tradition do not seem to have been preserved in the many surviving volumes of Mikyö Dorjé's collected works, but the questions are quoted in Sokdokpa's reply to them. For translations and discussions of a few of the Karmapa's comments and Sokdokpa's replies, see Karmay 1988, 181–82, 188–89, and 195.

14. See Ngawang Losang Gyatso, *Sunlight of the Doctrine of the Explication for Disciples*, 565–66.

15. See Ngawang Losang Gyatso, *Sunlight of the Doctrine of the Explication for Disciples*, 589.

16. There are two detailed yet sharply differing versions of these complicated events. Jamgön Ameshap ('Jam mgon A mes zhabs, 1597–1659), the grandson of Ngakchang Kunga Rinchen (Sngags 'chang Kun dga rin chen, 1517–84), emphasizes that Tsarchen and Kunga Rinchen had deep respect and admiration for each other. He says Tsarchen's biographers (the Dar ruler, his cousin, and an abbot of one of Tsarchen's monasteries in that region) were biased and their accounts untrustworthy. The Fifth Dalai Lama (basing his version on precisely the sources Jamgön Ameshap criticizes) harshly blames Kunga Rinchen for almost everything bad that occurred. See Jamgön Ameshap, *A Sun Illuminating All the Teachings of the Dharma Protectors*, vol. 2: 181–87, and Ngawang Losang Gyatso, *Sunlight of the Doctrine of the Explication for Disciples*, 535, 611–16.

This unfortunate conflict caused a schism between the masters of the Khön family at Sakya and the masters of Tsarchen's lineage that was not fully healed until almost two hundred years later, when the Sakya throne holder Gongma Kunga Lodrö (Gong ma Kun dga' blo gros, 1729–83) requested the transmission of crucial teachings such as the Lamdré, Nāro Khecarī, and the Dharma protectors from the Tsarpa master Kunga Lekpai Jungné (Kun dga' legs pa'i 'byung gnas, 1704–60). I first heard stories of these events from Dezhung Rinpoché in the late 1970s.

17. See Ngawang Losang Gyatso, *Sunlight of the Doctrine of the Explication for Disciples*, 623: *nga la yang dgra 'dra yod pas 'dul dgos pa yod gsung yang na so rgas pas mi yong 'dug pas nga'i dgra khyed slob ma rnams kyis 'dul dgos gsung/ ha cang dgra tshan che shos 'khor bar skyur mkhan dug lnga yin pas 'di 'dul ba yin mod gsung/ yang dug lnga med pa byas na ye shes lnga'i rgyu mi yong 'dug de yang mi yong 'dug gsungs*. The five poisons are desire, hatred, ignorance, jealousy, and greed, which are to be transformed into the five types of primordial awareness associated with the five buddha families.

18. See Ngawang Losang Gyatso, *Sunlight of the Doctrine of the Explication for Disciples*, 623–25.

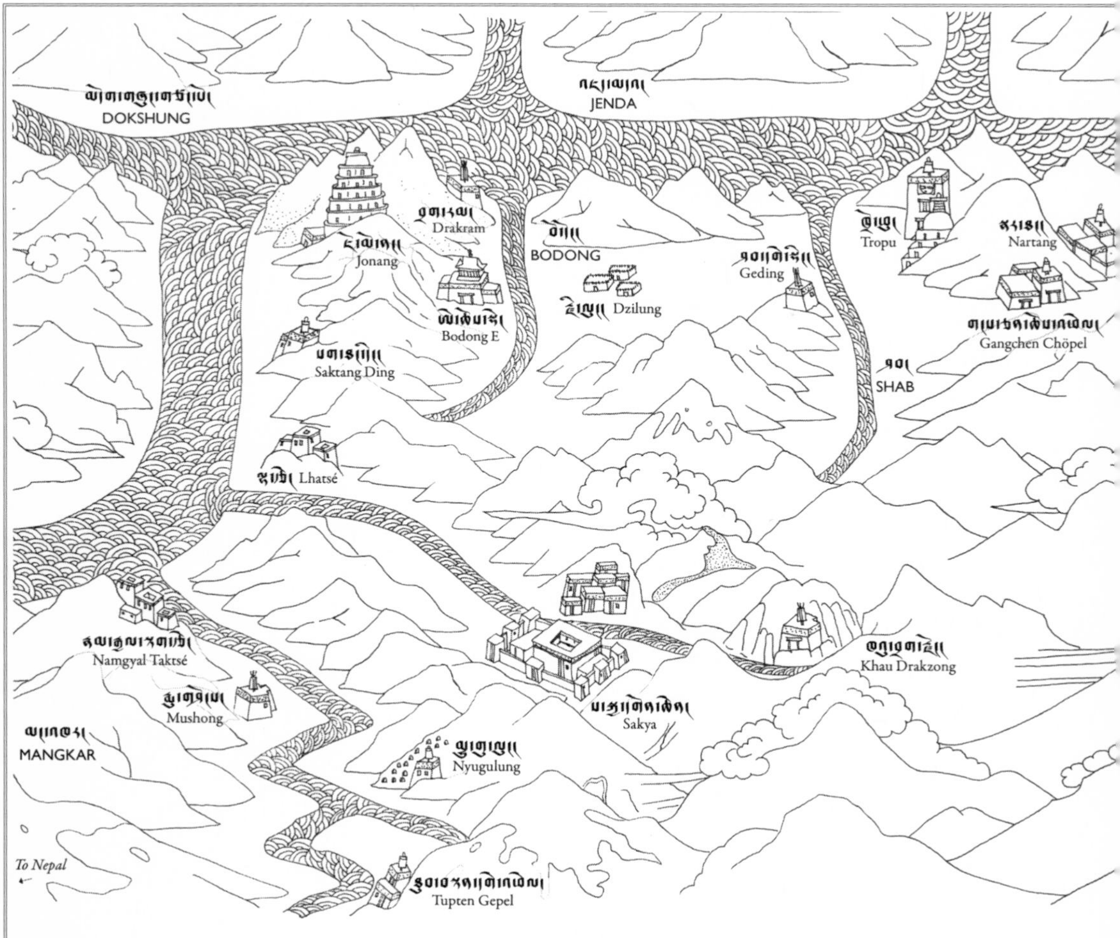
DOKSHUNG
JENDA
Drakram
Jonang
BODONG
Geding
Tropu
Nartang
Dzilung
Bodong E
Gangchen Chöpel
Saktang Ding
SHAB
Lhatsé
Namgyal Taktsé
Khau Drakzong
Mushong
Sakya
MANGKAR
Nyugulung
To Nepal
Tupten Gepel

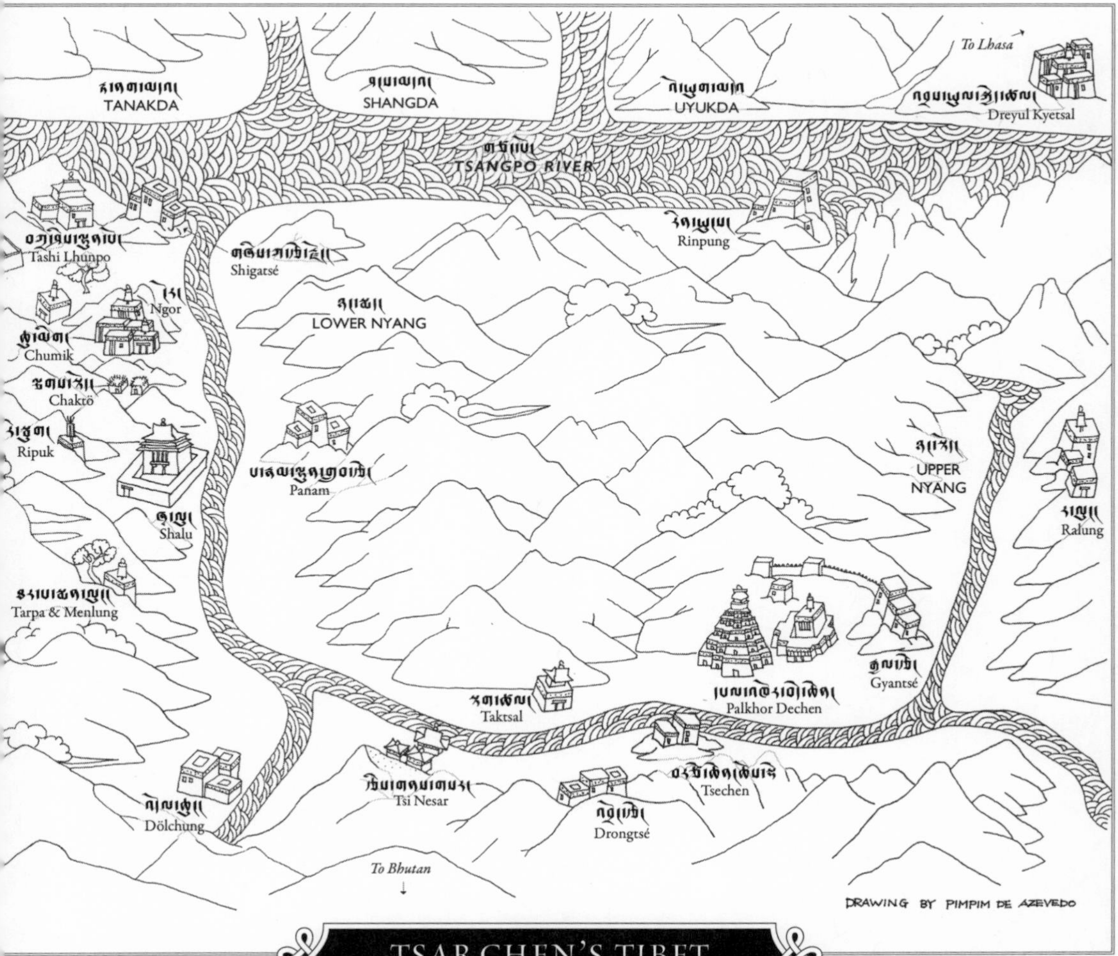

TSARCHEN'S TIBET

Celebration of the Cuckoo

by Tsarchen Losal Gyatso

1539

རང་གི་རྟོགས་བརྗོད་ལམ་སྐུ་དཔྱིད་ཀྱི་རྒྱལ་མོའི་དགའ་སྟོན་ཞེས་བྱ་བ་བཞུགས་སོ།

ན་མཿསརྦ་གུ་རུ་བུདྡྷ་བོ་དྷི་སཏྭ་བྷྱཿ

ཕྱི་ལྟར་ན་ཕྱོགས་མེད་ཀྱི་བནྡེ། ནང་ལྟར་ན་གསང་ཆེན་གྱི་སྔགས་འཆང་། གསང་བ་ལྟར་ན་རྗེ་བཙུན་རྡོ་རྗེ་འཆང་ཆེན་པོ་རྡོ་རིང་ཀུན་སྤངས་པ་ཞེས་ཡོངས་སུ་གྲགས་པ་དེའི་ཐུགས་གཉིས་སུ་མེད་པའི་ཡེ་ཤེས་དང་། ཆོས་དབྱིངས་བདེ་བ་ཆེན་པོའི་ངང་དུ་རོ་གཅིག་ཀྱང་། ཆོས་ཅན་གདངས་འགག་མེད་ཀྱི་རོལ་རྩེད་ཐ་དད་དུ་ཤར་བ། རྗེ་དེ་ཉིད་ཀྱི་ཞབས་ཀྱི་པདྨ་གཙུག་གིས་བསྟེན་ཅིང་། བཀའ་དྲིན་ཆེན་པོས་འཚོ་བའི་འཕྲིན་ལས་ཀྱི་འཁོར་ལོས་བསྒྱུར་བའི་བཀའ་འབབས་རིག་སྔགས་འཆང་བའི་བནྡེ་བློ་གསལ་རྒྱ་མཚོ་གྲགས་པ་རྒྱལ་མཚན་དཔལ་བཟང་པོ། ད་ལྟ་མིང་ཡོངས་སུ་གྲགས་པ་ཚར་པ་ཆོས་རྗེ། དོན་ལ་ཅི་མེད་ཀྱི་བྷུ་སུ་ཀུ། ཡུལ་ཕྱོགས་མེད་དུ་རྒྱུ་བའི་སྤྲང་པོ་ཡན་པ་བློ་བདེ་ཞེས་བྱ་བ་དེས། ཡུལ་འདར་སྟོད་མང་

Celebration of the Cuckoo

MY AUTOBIOGRAPHICAL SONG OF THE ROAD

Namaḥ sarva guru buddha bodhisattvabhyaḥ

Outwardly, I'm a homeless monk, inwardly, a mantra bearer of the great secret. Secretly, in the ecstatic sphere of the basic space of phenomena, I am identical with the nondual primordial awareness of the mind of that venerable lord, great Vajradhara, known everywhere as Doring Kunpangpa. And yet in the radiant, ceaseless play of phenomena, we appear different. With the crown of my head supporting the lotus at the feet of that very lord, the universal monarch of kindly nourishing deeds, I am his subject, a bearer of the mantras of pure awareness, the monk Losal Gyatso Drakpa Gyaltsen Palsangpo, now known everywhere by the name Dharma Lord Tsarpa. But really I'm just a poor lazy bum, that beggar called Carefree Vagabond, aimlessly roaming the land, one who displayed the miracle of birth in the Mangkar mansion of the region of upper Dar—although

མཁར་གྱི་ཕོ་བྲང་དུ་སྐྱེ་བ་མེད་པ་ལ་སྐྱེ་བའི་ཆོ་འཕྲུལ་བསྟན། གྲུམ་སྟོད་ཁའུའི་བྲག་ལ་སྒོམ་རྒྱུ་རྩོལ་ཙམ་མེད་པ་ལ་སྒོམ་པའི་རོ་མྱངས། རྒྱལ་ཁམས་ཕྱོགས་མེད་ཀྱི་བཞི་མདོར་རང་དོན་གྱི་དགོས་པ་ཅི་ཡང་མེད་བཞིན་དུ་ཉིན་མཚན་ཡད་ཡུད་དུ་འགྲོ་བའི་དགོས་དོན་མང་པོ་སྐྱོད་ཅིང་གནས་པ་ལས།

བྱེ་བྲག་ཏུ་རང་ལོ་སུམ་ཅུ་སོ་བརྒྱད་ཡན་ལ། ཡུལ་དབུས་ཀྱི་སྨན་ལྗོངས་སུ་ལན་གསུམ་ཕྱིན་པའི་དང་པོ། རྗེ་བཙུན་འཇམ་པའི་དབྱངས་ཀྱི་རྣམ་པར་སྤྲུལ་པ་རྗེ་ངག་དབང་གྲགས་པའི་ཞབས་ཕྱིར་འབྲངས་ཏེ་ཕྱིན་ནས་ལོ་བརྒྱད་ཙམ་བསྡད། བར་པ་ལ་ས་སྐྱ་པའི་བསྟན་པའི་སྦྱིན་བདག་སྤྲ་ར་བས་གསུང་ངག་བླ་མ་བརྒྱུད་པའི་གསེར་སྐུ་བཞེངས་པའི་རབ་གནས་ལ་ཕྱིན་ནས་ཟླ་བ་དྲུག་ཙམ་བསྡད་དེ་མགྱོགས་བསྐོར་བྱས། དེ་དག་གི་ལོ་རྒྱུས་རྣམས་བཤད་ན། དགའ་བ་ལ་བསམས་ན་ནམ་ལངས་པ་འདྲ་བ། སྐྱོ་བ་ལ་བསམས་ན་ས་རུབ་པ་འདྲ་བ། བཏང་སྙོམས་པ་བྱང་ཐང་སྐྱ་མོ་ལ་གར་བྱེད་པ་འདྲ་བ་ཇི་སྙེད་ཅིག་ཡོད་པ་ལབས་ཀྱང་སྤྲང་པོའི་གླུ་ལ་ཉན་མཁན་མེད་པས་དགོས་པ་ཆུང་བས་རྒྱབ་ཏུ་སྐྱུར་ལ་ཞོག

ལན་གསུམ་པ་རང་ལོ་སོ་བརྒྱད་པའི་དུས་སུ་ཕྱིན་ནས་ལོ་གཉིས་ཙམ་བསྡད་དུས་ཀྱི་འཕྲོས་གཏམ། ཡས་ཕྱིན་གྱི་ལམ་དུ་ཇི་ལྟར་བྱུང་བའི་ཚུལ་གྱི་རྟོགས་བརྗོད་ལམ་གླུ་དཔྱིད་ཀྱི་རྒྱལ་མོའི་དགའ་སྟོན། ཀུ་མུད་གསར་པ་ཁ་བྱེ་བ་འདྲ་བ་འདི་ཉིད་སྨྲས་པ་ལ་ཆེད་དུ་དགོས་པ་ཆེན་པོ་མི་འདུག་སྟེ། གསང་དགོས་པའི་མཚང་ཡང་མེད་པས། སྣང་བ་གདོང་འདེད་གཞིར་བཞག་ལ། ད་ལམ་ལབ་པ་ངོས་འདི་སྣང་བ་ལ་ཤར་བྱུང་བས་གསན་པ་ཞུ་ཞིག

དེ་ཡང་། དེ་གོང་ཕྱིན་དུས་གྲྭ་རིགས་སྦྱིན་བདག་སོ་སོར་ཡོད་པའི་ཁས་ལེན་ཡང་བྱས་

there is no birth; experienced the taste of meditation at Khau cliffs in upper Drüm—although there is not even an atom to meditate upon; and without any need from my own side, stayed at random crossroads in lower valleys of the country performing day and night many acts that passed in a blur.

Specifically, by age thirty-eight, I traveled three times to the herbal lands of the Ü region. The first was when I followed as an attendant of Lord Ngawang Drakpa, an emanation of the venerable lord Mañjughoṣa, and stayed for about eight years. The second was when I went for the consecration of the golden images of the lineal masters of the Teaching, which the Para patron of the Sakya doctrine had constructed, stayed for about six months, and made a quick tour. Were I to tell stories of those trips, if I think of the joy, it is like daybreak, if I think of the sorrow, like nightfall. Equanimity is like dancing on the pale northern steppes. But whatever I might say, no one listens to a beggar's song. So there's little need. Let's just drop it.

I went for a third time when I was thirty-eight years old and stayed for about two years. As a tale of that period, there's no special great need to speak this *Celebration of the Cuckoo: An Autobiographical Song of the Road*, which is like a blooming new moon-lily revealing just what happened on the road leading up there. But there is also no fault that needs to be kept secret. So, taking for granted my stubborn nature, please listen to this I now actually tell, because it is my impression of what happened.

Furthermore, when I went before, I had also made promises to visit individual monastic patrons. Later, insistent emissaries had regularly arrived up to the present. The time had also come to train several worthy students fit for training. And

ཡོད་པ་དང་། རྗེས་སུ་རིམ་པར་ནན་ཏན་གྱི་འབོད་མི་འཕྲལ་དུ་བྱུང་བ་དང་། འདུལ་བར་འོས་པའི་སྟོད་ལྷན་གྱི་གདུལ་བྱ་འགའ་ཞིག་ཀྱང་འདུལ་བའི་དུས་ལ་བབས་འདུག་ཅིང་། རང་ཉིད་ཀྱང་ཡུལ་ཕྱོགས་མེད་ཀྱི་བདུད་རྩི་བསྟེན་ན་ནང་དུ་སེམས་ཉིད་ལ་འགྱུར་བ་ཆེན་པོ་ཞིག་འོང་ཤས་ཆེ་བས།

དེ་སྐྱ་ཕྱིན་པའི་དུས། སྦྱིན་བདག་གི་རྟ་དྲིལ་གྱིས་བསྐྱིལ་བསུ་བྱས་པའི་ཚེ། རྟ་རྫི་དྲིལ་རྫི་མི་ངན་བསམ་པ་ཆུང་ཞིང་ལྟོགས་འདོད་ཆེ་བ་རྣམས་ཀྱི་ངོ་མི་ཟིན་བཞིན་དུ་འཛོན་དགོས་པ་དེ་ཞེ་སུན་ལ་སྐབས་སུ་མི་བབ་པ་ཞིག་འོང་གིན་འདུག་པ་དང་ཁྱད་པར་ལམ་བར་རྣམས་སུ་ཡང་སྔར་ཆོས་འབྲེལ་ཡོད་པ་དང་། ད་ཆོས་ཞུ་འདོད་ཀྱི་བླ་མ་མཇལ་བ། གནས་བཟང་པོ་དང་རྟེན་ཁྱད་པར་ཅན་མཇལ་བ་སོགས་དགོས་དོན་ཐམས་ཅད་བློས་བཏང་ནས། བདེ་གཟར་ཆེན་པོ་འབྲུག་ཁ་མའི་གསེར་ཡིག་པ་བཞིན་དུ་ནམ་ལངས་ས་ཏུབ་དྲིལ་ཁལ་གྱི་རྗེས་ལ། ལམ་གཞུང་བསྲངས་ནས་ཐལ་མར་རྒྱུག་དགོས་པ་དེ་ཡེ་ཡིད་ལ་མི་འབབ་པ་ཞིག་བྱུང་བས།

བྱ་བྲལ་འགྲོས་ཀྱི་འགྲོ་བར་བརྩམས་ཏེ་ཕག་གི་ལོ་ཏོར་ཟླ་ལྔ་པའི་དུས། ས་གཞི་རྣམས་མ་རྒད་གསར་པས་བྱུགས་པ་ལྟར་རྩྭ་སྔོན་གྱིས་སྔོ་འཛམ་དུ་གྱུར་ཅིང་། ཨིནྡྲ་ནཱི་ལའི་རྒྱ་མཚོ་སློ་བུར་དུ་རྫོལ་བ་ལྟར་ཆུ་བོ་དང་ཆུ་ཕྲན་མཐའ་དག་རབ་ཏུ་རྒྱས་ཤིང་རླབས་ཕྲེང་གིས་མཛེས་པའི་ལྷུ་བའི་འཇུམ་དཀར་ཕྱོགས་བརྒྱར་རྒོད་པ་སྐྱེ་བོ་རྣམས་དཔྱིད་ཀྱི་དུས་སྟོན་བཟང་པོ་ལ་བབས་པས་དགའ་ཞིང་ཆགས་པའི་རྣམ་འགྱུར་ཤས་ཆེར་སྟོན་པའི་རི་ཀླུང་ཀུན་ཁྱབ་པར་ཀླུ་དབྱངས་དང་གཏོད་སྒྲ་འབྲེལ་མར་རྒྱུ་བའི་ཚེ།

if I resorted to the nectar of being homeless myself, a great change would most likely occur in the essence of mind within.

During the previous trips, when the patron's horses and donkeys had escorted me, the horsemen and donkey tenders were bad, small-minded men with great appetites, whom I had to accept as superiors (while not really doing so). That irritated me and became an inappropriate situation. In particular, at points along the way I had to abandon all my goals, such as visiting masters with whom I had previous Dharma connections and those from whom I wished to now request Dharma, as well as visiting good places and exceptional sacred objects. Like an imperial envoy at the outbreak of hostilities during a great conflict, I had to rush straight down the main roads and pathways behind the donkey-loads from daybreak to nightfall, which was extremely unpleasant.

So. We began to travel at the pace of mendicants. During the fifth moon of the pig year the fresh grass had changed the landscape to a gentle green as if anointed with new emeralds. All the rivers and streams were fully swollen, like a sea of sapphires suddenly welling up, beautiful with garlands of waves whose white foamy smiles laughed in a hundred directions. It was time for the good festival of spring, so people were acting joyful and passionate, moving about with ballads and the sounds of laughter filling by turns all the mountains and valleys.

With the messengers of invitation, there were about fifteen of us, teacher and students all in the prime of life, not too old or too young, wearing only

གདན་འདྲེན་གྱི་ཕོ་ཉ་དང་བཅས་པའི་ངེད་དཔོན་སློབ་ལྔ་ཕྲག་གསུམ་ཙམ་ཡོད་པ་ཐམས་ཅད་ཧ་ཅང་རྒན་པ་དང་གཞོན་པ་མ་ཡིན་པར་ལང་ཚོ་དར་ལ་བབ་པ། དགེ་སྦྱོང་ལ་འོས་པའི་ཆ་ལུགས་ངུར་སྨྲིག་གི་རྒྱལ་མཚན་ཞེ་གཅིག་པ། ཆེད་དུ་སྤོང་བ་ལྷུར་ལེན་པའི་མཚོན་བྱེད་རས་དཀར་གྱི་ལྷོག་པ་གངས་རིའི་དུམ་བུ་ཚལ་དུ་ཆད་པ་འདྲ་བ་རེ་དང་། སྣ་དབྱུག་དཀར་པོ་དུང་གི་ཚུགས་ཤིང་ལྟ་བུ་རེ། བསམ་གཏན་གྱི་འཕོལ་ཆུང་ཁ་གང་མ་གྲུ་ཟུར་མ་ཉམས་པ་རེ། གྲུ་ཆུང་དང་གྲུ་ཕད་ཟུར་གསུམ་པདྨ་རྣ་ག་དང་པདྨའི་རྩ་བ་ཐགས་སུ་བཏགས་པ་ལྟ་བུ་རེ། སྐལ་ལྡན་རྗེས་སུ་འཛིན་པའི་སླད་དུ་སྙན་བརྒྱུད་ཟབ་མོའི་བེའུ་བུམ་པོ་ཏི་རེ་དང་བཅས་པ་ཁུར། ཁོ་བོ་ཅག་རྐང་འགྲོས་ཀྱིས་བུལ་བས། རྟ་སྔོན་པོ་བརྟན་བརླིང་འཛོམ་པ་སྣ་སྦྲབ་ལ་སོགས་པ་དཀྱུས་ཐུབ་པ་ཞིག་ལ་ཞོན། ཐུབ་པས་དབྱར་གྱི་རས་ཆེན་གནང་བ་དང་མཐུན་པའི་ཆར་སྐྱོབ་ཀྱི་རས་ནམ་ཐང་ཡུག་པོ་ཆེ་མུ་མེན་གྱི་མཐའ་འཛག་བཏང་བ་ལྟ་བུ་ཞིག་གྱོན།

མང་མཁར་ཐུབ་བསྟན་དགེ་འཕེལ་གྱི་དགོན་པ་ནས་ཆས་ཏེ། རང་གི་བསྡི་གནས་སུ་ཙུང་ཟད་ངལ་གསོས། འདར་སྟོད་རྣམ་རྒྱལ་སྟག་རྩེའི་ཕོ་བྲང་གི་མདུན་སར་མཆོད་རྟེན་གྱི་རབ་གནས་དང་དགའ་སྟོན་བསྒྲུབས་ཏེ་རིམ་པར་ཆས་པ་ནི་འདི་ལྟར་རོ།

ཡིད་འོང་མཚོ་ཆེན་ངོགས་སུ་ཆས་པ་ཡི།།
དཔལ་ལྡན་དང་པའི་རྒྱལ་པོ་འདབ་བཟང་དབང་།།
ངུར་པ་བྱེ་བས་བསྐོར་བའི་མཛེས་སྡུག་ནི།།
མཁའ་ལ་ལི་ཁྲིའི་རྡུལ་དམར་འཁྲིགས་པ་ལྟར།།

the saffron victory banner of dress befitting ordained persons. Symbolizing our acceptance of deliberate renunciation, we each carried a little tent of white cotton, like the shattered shard of a glacial mountain; a white rattan staff, like a tent pole of conch shell; a small meditation cushion; a square rug with untrimmed edges; a pouch and a three-cornered sack, as if woven of rubies and lotus roots; and a special volume of the profound oral transmission with which to grace fortunate people. My pace on foot would have been too slow, so I rode a dependable fine gray horse that could handle the usual saddle, bridle, and so on. In keeping with the large summer cloak the Sage allowed, we wore, for protection from the rain, cloaks of whole serge seemingly bordered with lapis lazuli.

We set out from Tupten Gepel Monastery in Mangkar and rested a little at my family home. In the assembly hall of the palace of Namgyal Taktsé in upper Dar, we completed the consecration of a stūpa and held a celebration. Our gradual departure was like this:

> The exquisite beauty
> of the glorious swan king,
> avian lord surrounded by
> ten million ruddy sheldrakes
> departing from the shore
> of a great enchanting lake,
> is like the sky laced with
> powder of red lead.

དེ་བཞིན་བསྟན་དང་འགྲོ་བའི་དོན་ཆེན་ལ།།
རིངས་པར་ཆས་པའི་རྣལ་འབྱོར་ཀུ་སཱ་ལི།།
ངུར་སྨྲིག་འཛིན་པའི་སློབ་འཁོར་དང་བཅས་པ།།
ཡུལ་དབུས་འཛིན་མའི་སྨན་ལྗིངས་ཡངས་པར་ཆས།།

གང་དེ་མཐོང་བའི་སྐལ་བཟང་གཞོན་ནུ་རྣམས།།
འདི་སྐྱིད་ཕྱི་མ་བདེ་བའི་རྣམ་ཐར་ཅན།།
འདི་འདྲའི་རྗེས་སུ་ང་ཡང་ཁྲིད་ན་སྙམ།།
ཡིད་ཀྱིས་རེ་སྨོན་ཅི་ཡང་འདེབས་པར་བྱེད།།

དེའི་ནུབ་ཧ་ཅང་མི་རིང་པའི་གྲོང་ཁྱེར་དོན་འགྲུབ་གླིང་ཞེས་བྱ་བར་སྐྱིད་ཚལ་ལྗོན་ཤིང་གི་དོ་ར་འཁྲིགས་པ་ཞིག་འདུག་པ་དེར་ཕྱོག་གྲྭ་རྣམས་ཕྲིན་དཀར་གྱི་འཕྲེང་བ་ཚར་དུ་དངར་བ་ལྟར་བརྒྱབ། ཆོས་སྤྱོད་ཀྱི་རིམ་པ་འབྲུག་གི་སྒྲ་ལྟར་དུ་ལྡིར། རྒྱ་ཇ་བཟང་པོ་ངར་དང་འཇོམ་པའི་བཏུང་བ་དབྱར་གྱི་རྒྱ་མཚོ་ལྟར་ཆལ་ཆིལ་དུ་ལོངས་སྤྱོད་ཅིང་གནས་པའི་ཚེ། དེའི་དགོན་པར་ཆོས་རྗེའི་དྲུང་གིས་ངེད་དཔོན་སློབ་འགའ་གདན་དྲངས་གཞིས་ལེན་ཤངས་ལེན་བཟབས་མ་མཛད། ནང་སོ་དང་སྤར་འདྲིས་ཀྱི་གྲྭ་པ་རྣམས་ཀྱིས་ཀྱང་ཇ་འདྲེན་སོགས་ལེགས་ཚོགས་ཀྱི་རྟེན་འབྲེལ་ཐོག་མར་འགྲིག་པ་བྱུང་།

So, too, for the great
benefit of the doctrine
and living beings, a mendicant
yogin swiftly departed
with a circle of saffron-clad
students, setting off
for the wide herbal lands
of the region of Ü.

Seeing him, fortunate
young people expressed
various hopes and aspirations,
thinking, "May I also
be guided in the footsteps
of one like this, whose way
is happy in this life and will be
pleasant in the next."

That night, not far away in a village called Döndrup Ling, there was a dense grove of trees with an open area where we pitched our tents like a garland of white clouds arranged in a row. The stages of the Dharma liturgy roared like thunder. As we sat enjoying a drink of fine and strong yet fragrant Chinese

དེ་སྟ་ཡན་ཆར་དཀོན་ཙམ་ཡོད་པ་ལ། དེ་རྗེས་ངེད་དཔོན་སློབ་རྣམས་སོ་སོར་དགོངས་ཐུན་གྱི་རིམ་གཉིས་ཀྱི་རྣལ་འབྱོར་ལ་འཇུག་པར་རྩོམ་པ་ན། ཕྱོགས་ཐ་གྲུ་ནས་ཆར་སྤྲིན་དཔལ་བུ་གཏིབས། འབྲུག་སྒྲ་ཟབ་མོའི་སྒྲ་དབྱངས་དང་བཅས་པའི་ཆར་གྱི་རྒྱུན་ཆེན་པོ་བབས་པས། འབྲུ་བཅུད་རྣམས་རབ་ཏུ་སོས་ཤིང་སྐྱེ་བོ་རྣམས་ཡིད་དགའ་བདེས་འཚོ་བར་གྱུར་ཏོ།

ཧྲུ་སུ་ཀུ་དེ་ལམ་དུ་ཆས་པའི་ཚེ།།
དེ་ཡི་གཙུག་རྒྱན་རྗེ་བཙུན་ཁའུ་པའི།།
ཐུགས་རྗེའི་དགེ་མཚན་འོད་ཟེར་སྟོང་འཕྲོས་པས།།
རྒྱ་མཚོའི་ཀླུ་རྣམས་དགའ་བའི་ཟློས་གར་ལས།།
ཕྱོགས་ཀུན་ཆར་སྤྲིན་གསར་པས་ཆེད་དུ་གཏིབས།།
སྤྲིན་ཏུམ་ནང་ནས་འབྲུག་སྒྲ་དཔལ་གྱིས་སྒྲོད།།

གློག་ཕྲེང་གཞོན་ནུའི་གོ་སྐབས་དབྱེ་བ་ཡི།།
ཡིད་བཞིན་སྤྲོས་ཆུའི་ཆར་ཆེན་དེང་འདིར་བབས།།

tea rippling like a summer lake, the honorable Dharma lord at that monastery invited several of us, teacher and students, and held a lavish welcoming reception. The steward, and monks I knew from before, also served tea and so forth, so an auspicious combination of good things occurred at the beginning.

Before that, rain had been a bit scarce, but after that, when we teacher and students began to engage in the yoga of two stages during our individual evening sessions, rain clouds softly clustered from valleys in every direction. When great sheets of rain fell with a deep rumble of thunder, the sprouts of grain were fully nurtured, and the minds of people were nourished with joy and happiness.

> When that lazy bum
> set out upon the path, as a
> good sign of the compassion
> of his crown ornament,
> the venerable lord of Khau,
> a thousand light rays shone,
> and from the joyous musical
> drama of the nāgas of the sea,
> new rain clouds clustered
> in all directions.
>
> Thunder chuckled
> from the wombs of clouds.

ལོ་ཏོག་རྩི་ཤིང་ཉི་གཞོན་གྱིས་སྤེ་བའི།།
པདྨོ་ཇི་བཞིན་ཕྱོགས་བཅུར་འཛུམ་དཀར་གཡོ།།

མི་རྣམས་སྦྲང་རྩིས་སྨྱོས་པའི་བུང་བ་བཞིན།།
རབ་ཏུ་དགའ་བའི་དར་དིར་གླུ་དབྱངས་ལེན།།

སང་ཉིན་སྔ་བར་ཆས་ནས་ལྷགས་ལ་ཞེས་བྱའི་ལ་བརྒལ་ནས་རིམ་པར་བརྒྱུད། ལྷགས་ཐང་གི་མདའ་ཕྱུག་པོ་ཤར་པ་ཟེར་བའི་ཁྱིམ་བདག་དད་པ་ཅན་ཞིག་གི་ལྷུང་ར་གླུ་སྡིངས་ཤིག་འདུག་པར་བསྡད། དེར་ཟླ་བ་ཡར་ངོའི་ཚེས་བཅོ་ལྔ་རྗེ་བླ་མའི་ཚེས་མཆོད་ཀྱི་སྐབས་སུ་བབ་བྱུང་བས། བླ་མ་མཆོད་ཆོག་རྒྱས་པར་བྱས་སྦྱིན་བདག་དེས་ཀྱང་བསྙེན་བཀུར་འབུལ་བ་སོགས་ཡང་དག་བྱུང་།

Heralded by fresh
garlands of lightning,
here today a great rain
of wish-fulfilling perfume fell.

Just like lotuses opened
by the young sun, the bright
smiles of crops and plants
flickered in the ten directions.

And people sang songs,
gleefully buzzing
like honey-crazed bees.

We sat off early the next morning, crossed the pass called Chakla, and gradually continued. In the lower valley of Chaktang we stayed in a raised hollow of willow trees belonging to a faithful householder called Chukpo Sharpa. The occasion of the anniversary of my lord master fell on the fifteenth day of the waxing moon there, so we performed the extensive rite of offering to the masters. That patron also provided perfect hospitality and so forth.

སང་ཚ་བའི་སྙིང་དུ་བླ་མ་ཞང་དགོན་པ་བའི་སྒྲུབ་གནས། རྗེ་བཙུན་ས་སྐྱ་པ་ཆེན་པོའི་གསུང་ངག་རིན་པོ་ཆེ་གསན་པའི་ཡུལ་སག་ཐང་དིང་ཞེས་བྱ་བར་སླེབས། དེའི་གཙུག་ལག་ཁང་མཆོད་རྟེན་ཆོས་ཁྲི་དང་བཅས་པ་མཇལ། ཕྱག་མཆོད་སྨོན་ལམ་གསོལ་གདབ་བྱས་ཏེ།

དཔལ་རྫོ་མོ་ནང་གི་རི་ཁྲོད་ཆེན་པོར་སླེབས། དེའི་ནུབ་སྐུ་འབུམ་ཐང་དུ་ཟློག་གྲྭ་བྱས་བསྡད་པས། དེར་གནས་མཇལ་ལ་འོངས་པའི་ཕྱོགས་ཀྱི་སྐྱ་སེར་ཕོ་མོ་མང་པོ་འདུག་པ་རྣམས་ཀྱིས། ངེད་དཔོན་སློབ་ལ་ལྟད་མོ་དག་སྣང་སྐོར་བ་ཆོས་འབྲེལ་ཞུ་བ་སོགས་མང་པོ་བྱུང་།

སང་སྤུ་དོ་སྐུ་འབུམ་མཐོང་གྲོལ་ཆེན་མོ། སྦྱོར་དྲུག་བརྒྱུད་པའི་ལྷ་ཁང་སོགས་མཇལ། རི་ཁྲོད་ལ་རྒྱང་བལྟས་བྱས་པས་བློ་འགྲོ་ཞིང་ཡིད་འཕྲོག་པ། སྔོན་གྱི་དམ་པ་རྣམས་ཀྱིས་འདི་ལྟ་བུའི་གནས་སུ་སྒྲུབ་གྲྭའི་རྒྱུན་བཙུགས། སྐྱེ་བོ་མང་པོ་ཐར་པའི་ལམ་ལ་འགོད་པར་མཛད་པ་ཆེས་ཆེར་ངོ་མཚར་ཞིང་རྨད་དུ་བྱུང་བའི་རྣམ་ཐར་དུ་འདུག ཁོ་བོ་ཅག་ཀྱང་འདི་ལྟ་བུའི་དབེན་གནས་ཤིག་ཏུ་བྱང་ཆུབ་སྒྲུབ་པ་ཞིག་ནམ་འོང་སྙམ་པ་སྙིང་གི་དཀྱིལ་དུ་ལྷང་ལྷང་བའི་དག་སྣང་བྱུང་ངོ་།

At mealtime the next day we arrived at the place known as Saktang Ding, the meditation site of the master Shang Gönpawa, where the great venerable lord of Sakya received the Precious Teaching. We visited its temple, stūpa, and Dharma throne and made prostrations, offerings, prayers, and supplications.

Then we arrived at the great hermitage of glorious Jonang. That night we pitched our tents and stayed on the plateau around the stūpa. Many lay and ordained men and women had come from different directions to visit the place there. With deep appreciation, they viewed us teacher and students as a spectacle, and many made circumambulations, requested Dharma connections, and so on.

The next morning we visited such sites as the great Stūpa that Liberates on Sight and the temple of the lineage of the Six-Branch Yoga. When I gazed from afar at the hermitages, my mind went out to them and I was enthralled. "The excellent beings of the past established a continuing meditation center in a place such as this," I thought. "Placing many people on the path of freedom, their way of life was so amazing and so incredible. When will I also practice for enlightenment in an isolated place such as this?" Distinctly vivid deep appreciation dawned in the center of my heart.

ཨེ་མ་ནགས་རྒྱལ་སྨན་བཙུན་དབང་མོའི་རི།།
རི་ངོས་ཚང་ཚོང་འཁྲིགས་པའི་ནགས་ཀྱི་ཁྲོད།།
ཁྲོད་ཡངས་རྗེ་བའི་སྤྲེལ་ཚུང་སྐྱིད་པའི་ནང་།།
ནང་དེར་བྱང་ཆུབ་སྒྲུབ་པའི་སྐལ་བཟང་ཚོ།།
མཐོང་བའི་མོད་ལ་ཡིད་ནི་ཟ་ཟིར་གྱུར།།

བདག་ཀྱང་ནམ་ཞིག་འདི་འདྲའི་སྐལ་བཟང་ཞིག།
ཅིས་ཀྱང་བསྒྲུབ་སྙམ་སྙིང་གི་གསེབ་དབྲག་ཏུ།།
འགྱུར་མེད་དམ་བཅའི་ཕུར་པ་བརྟན་པོར་བཙུགས།།

Pema Wangchen Yangsang Tröpa

E Ma! Nakgyal,
the mentsun queen's
mountain; mountainside
forest thickly tangled within;
within it, little stone huts,
pleasant and spacious inside;
inside which the fortunate practiced
for enlightenment; seeing whom,
I became anxious.

Thinking, "I too
must someday practice
with good fortune like this,"
I firmly drove the stake
of an immutable oath
into the core of my heart.

དེ་ནས་མདའ་སྐོར་བྱས། བྲག་རམ་ཆོས་སྡེའི་མགོན་ཁང་མཇལ། གནོད་སྦྱིན་ཆེན་པོ་ལ་སྙན་དར་གསོལ་མཆོད་འཕྲིན་བཅོལ་དང་བཅས་པ་རྒྱས་པར་བྱས། བྲག་རམ་སློབ་དཔོན་པས་གདན་དྲངས། ཛ་འདྲེན་རས་དཀར་གྱི་ཕྱག་རྟེན་དང་བཅས་པ་ཕུལ། གནོད་སྦྱིན་གྱི་ཆོས་སྐོར་ཞུ་བའི་སྙན་གསན་ཕབ། རྗེས་སུ་དེ་ལྟར་བྱེད་པ་ཁས་བླངས།

དེ་དང་ཁད་ཉེ་བའི་ཆུ་མོ་ལུང་གི་དགོན་པ་ན་གྲུབ་པ་མཆོག་གི་དབང་པོ་འབྲུལ་ཞིག་རཏྣ་བྷ་དྲ་བཞུགས་པའི་དྲུང་དུ་མཇལ། དེ་ནུབ་ཚོགས་ཀྱི་འཁོར་ལོ་དང་བཅས་པའི་སྒོ་ནས་བཅོམ་ལྡན་འདས་པདྨ་དབང་ཆེན་ཡང་གསང་ཁྲོས་པ་ཁྲག་འཐུང་ལྷ་དགུའི་དབང་། དེའི་ཚེ་དབང་། བཀའ་སྲོད་གིང་ལྔ་གཟའ་གདོང་གི་སྲོག་དབང་བཀའ་གཏད་དང་བཅས་པ་ཞུས།

སང་འགྲོ་ཁར་ངེད་དཔོན་སློབ་ཐམས་ཅད་ཀྱིས་ལྷན་ཅིག་ཏུ་སློབ་དཔོན་ཆེན་པོ་པདྨ་འབྱུང་གནས་ཀྱི་སྒོ་ནས་བླ་མའི་རྣལ་འབྱོར་ཞུས། དེའི་ཚེ་རྗེ་བླ་མ་འབྲུལ་ཞིག་གི་སྒྲུད་པས་ཧཱུྃ་རིང་ཧཱུྃ་ཐུང་གི་གདངས་དབྱངས་གར་སྐབས་ངེད་ཀྱི་གྲྭ་པ་རྣམས་ལ་བཀའ་བསྐྱོན་དང་ཐུགས་འདོགས་སྤེལ་བའི་ཏུར་སྒྲུད་མང་པོ་མཛད་ཀྱི་འདུག་པས་ཁོང་ཚོ་ཐམས་ཅད་དང་པ་སྐྱིས། འཇིག་རྟེན་ཆོས་བརྒྱད་མེད་པའི་བླ་མ་ཟེར་ན་འདི་འདྲ་ཞིག་འོང་བ་ཡིན་ཟེར་ཞིང་གདའ།

Then we toured the lower valley. We visited the protector's chapel of Drakram Abbey, presented ceremonial scarves to the great yakṣa, and made extensive supplications and offerings along with invoking his actions. The teacher of Drakram invited us, served tea, and offered a gift of white cotton cloth. He made a formal request for the Dharma cycle of the yakṣa. I agreed to do so later.

At nearby Chumolung Monastery we visited the powerful, sublime adept for whom confusion has vanished, Ratnabhadra. That evening, in the context of a ritual feast, I requested the initiation of the nine blood-drinking deities of the blessed one, Pema Wangchen Yangsang Tröpa, his longevity initiation, and the life-force initiation and bestowal of authority for the guardians, the five emissaries and Rāhula.

As we left the next morning, we teacher and students all requested together a guruyoga of the great teacher Padmasambhava. At that time, when the lord master was performing the dance movements and melodic tunes of the long *hūṃ* and the short *hūṃ* with the conduct of one for whom confusion has vanished, engaging in much impulsive behavior, alternately scolding and acting affectionate toward my monks, they all became faithful, saying that if one were to speak of a master without the eight worldly concerns, he would be like this.

བླ་ལུང་རི་བོའི་སྒོ་ལ་འབྲུལ་ཞིག་རྗེ།།
ཀུན་བཟང་དགོངས་པའི་བཅུད་ཀྱིས་སྨྱོས་པ་དེས།།
གར་དགུའི་རོལ་རྩེད་ཧཱུྃ་སྒྲ་སྒྲོག་པའི་ཚེ།།
སྐལ་ལྡན་སྙིང་ལ་འདོད་འཛོའི་བཀའ་དྲིན་སྦྱིན།།

དེ་ནས་པོ་དོང་ཕུན་ཚོགས་རབ་བརྟན་གྱི་ཕོ་བྲང་ན། རྗེ་བཙུན་རྡོ་རྗེ་འཆང་ཆེན་པོ་མཁས་དང་གྲུབ་པའི་དབང་པོ་ཀུན་དགའི་མཚན་ཅན་བཞུགས་པའི་ཞབས་དྲུང་དུ་མཇལ། ངོས་ཀྱི་དཔལ་ཀྱི་རྡོ་རྗེའི་རས་བྲིས་ཀྱི་དཀྱིལ་འཁོར་དུ་དབང་བཞི་རྫོགས་པར་ཞུས། ངེད་དཔོན་སློབ་ཐམས་ཅད་ཐུན་མོང་དུ་གསེར་གཡབས་ཟེར་བའི་འབྲུམས་གྲྭ་ཞིག་འདུག་པ་དེར་ཕེབས། གདན་ཁྲི་ཤིན་ཏུ་མཐོ་བ་ལ་བཞུགས་ནས་སྐུའི་གཟི་བརྗིད་ཉི་ཟླ་ཟིལ་གྱིས་གནོན་ནུས་པ་ཙམ། གསུང་གི་གདངས་འབྲུག་ལྟར་ལྡིར་བཞིན་པས་རོལ་མོ་བཟང་པོ་འཁྲོལ་བ་དང་བཅས་ཚེ་དཔག་མེད་གྲུབ་རྒྱལ་ལུགས་ཀྱི་ཚེ་དབང་བཀའ་དྲིན་བསྐྱངས། ཁོ་བོ་རང་གིས་སྤར་ཕུལ་བའི་དབང་དྲིལ་ཤིང་ཁྲུལ་མས་གཙོ་བྱས་ཟང་ཟིང་གི་གནང་སྦྱིན་བཟང་པོའང་གནང་།

ངེད་རང་ནི་རྗེ་བཙུན་རྡོ་རིང་པ་ཆེན་པོ་ཆོས་དབྱིངས་སུ་གཤེགས་རྗེས་རྗེ་འདི་ཉིད་བླ་མའི་གཙོ་བོ་ཡིན་ཞིང་། རྡོ་རྗེ་འཆང་དངོས་ཀྱི་འདུ་ཤེས་ཡོད་པས་དད་པ་དང་སྤྲོ་བ་ཅིག་ཅར་བྱུང་། གྲྭ་པ་རྣམས་ནི་ཏ་ཅང་མཇལ་དཀའ་ཞིང་གཟི་བརྗིད་ཆེ་བ་ཙམ་འདུག་ངེད་

When on Mount Lalung's peak,
that lord for whom confusion
has vanished, crazed by the nutrient
of Samantabhadra's intent, playfully
enjoyed the nine dances, chanting
the sounds of *hūṃ*, the hearts of
the fortunate were granted the favor
of having their wishes fulfilled.

Then we visited the venerable lord, great Vajradhara, the powerful expert and realized being named Kunga, who was staying in the Puntsok Rabten palace of Bodong. I requested the complete four initiations in my painted cloth maṇḍala of glorious Hevajra. All of us, teacher and students, went together to that enclosed courtyard called Seryab. Seated on a very high throne, his physical dignity nearly able to eclipse the sun and moon, and with a tone of voice roaring like thunder (together with the playing of fine music), he favored us with the Amitāyus longevity initiation in the tradition of the Queen of Adepts. He also gave fine material gifts, the foremost being the initiation bell in a wooden case that I had previously offered.

For me, after the great venerable lord Doringpa passed into the basic space of phenomena, this very lord had been my chief master. Because I had the perception that he was actually Vajradhara, faith and delight instantly arose. But for

རང་གྲྭ་པ་རྣམས་ཀྱིས་བླ་མ་ཆོས་རྗེ་དཀའ་བཞི་པ་དེ་འདྲ་བ་ཞིག་ཡོང་བ་ཡིན་ཟེར་བ་ལ། ངེད་ཀྱིས་དེ་འདྲ་མ་ཟེར་རྗེ་འདི་པ་དིང་སང་གཟུར་གནས་ཀྱིས་བལྟས་ན་ས་སྐྱ་པའི་སྔགས་འཆང་ཀུན་གྱི་གཙོ་བོ། ངེད་རང་བདག་ཆེན་རྡོ་རྗེ་འཆང་ཆེན་པོའི་བརྒྱུད་འཛིན་རྣམས་ཀྱི་གཙུག་གི་ནོར་བུ། ཁྱད་པར་ངེད་རང་གི་བླ་མའི་གཙོ་བོ་རྡོ་རྗེ་འཆང་དངོས་དང་ཞལ་མི་གཉིས་པ་ཞིག་ཡིན་ཐག་ཆོད་པས། སོ་སོར་སྙིང་ནས་གསོལ་བ་ཐོབ། བྱིན་རླབས་ཁྱད་པར་ཅན་འཇུག་ངེས་པའི་ཁག་འཁུར་བ་ཡིན། འཕྲུལ་ཆེ་ཁྱད་ཆེ་བ་ཅམ་རྗེ་ལ་ཆོས་བརྒྱུད་ཀྱི་རྟོག་པ་ཅི་མངའ། སྨིན་བདག་སྟོབས་ལྡན་གྱི་ཞབས་ཏོག་ལ་དམིགས་པ་ཡིན་མོད་བྱས།

དེ་མཐུན་གནས་གསར་ནས་ནང་སོ་ཞལ་ངོ་རྣམས་ཀྱིས་ཀྱང་བསྙེན་བཀུར་ཤངས་ལེན་ཡང་དག་མཛད་དོ།

རྣམ་རྒྱལ་རབ་བརྟན་རྒྱལ་པོའི་ཕོ་བྲང་ན།།
ཆོས་ཀྱི་རྒྱལ་པོ་རྗེ་བཙུན་ཀུན་དགའི་མཚན།།
འཇིགས་མེད་སེང་གེའི་ཁྲི་ལ་འགྱིང་བཞིན་དུ།།
ངེས་དོན་ཟབ་མོའི་ངང་ནས་མ་གཡོས་པའི།།
ཞལ་བཟང་སྟོན་གྱི་ཟླ་ཤེལ་ལྟ་བུ་མཐོང་།།

ཞབས་ཀྱི་པདྨ་གཙུག་གི་རྒྱན་དུ་བླངས།།
གསང་ཆེན་བདུད་རྩིས་སྙིང་ལ་བདེ་བ་ཐོབ།།

monks, he was extremely difficult to meet and his dignity was formidable. My own monks said, "A master who is a Dharma lord of the four basic treatises can become like this." But I said, "Don't speak like that. If viewed impartially, this lord is nowadays the chief of all Sakya mantra bearers. He is the crown jewel of the holders of our lineage from Dakchen, great Vajradhara. In particular, he is the chief of my masters, and I am certain that his face is not different than that of Vajradhara himself. So you should each make heartfelt supplications. I guarantee that an exceptional blessing will certainly enter you. Any thought the lord has of the eight worldly concerns is just of great immediate importance and is surely intended for the service of a powerful patron."

In accordance with that, the governor and nobles from Nesar also offered perfect hospitality and a reception.

> In the royal palace
> of Namgyal Rabten I saw,
> like a crystal autumn moon,
> the fine face of the king of Dharma,
> the venerable lord named Kunga,
> majestic on a throne of fearless lions,
> yet never straying from the sphere
> of profound definitive meaning.
>
> The lotus at his feet
> I took as an ornament
> for the crown of my head.

ཀྭ་ཡེ་གྲོགས་དག་ཚུ་གཏེར་ཁ་དོག་ལ།།
མ་འཛིགས་དད་པའི་གཟིངས་སུ་ཞུགས་ཤིག་དང་།།

བཤེས་གཉེན་དམ་པའི་དེད་དཔོན་བཀའ་དྲིན་གྱིས།།
དངོས་གྲུབ་ནོར་བུ་ཐོབ་པར་ཐེ་ཚོམ་མེད།།

ས་སྙིང་འདི་ན་རྗེ་བཙུན་ས་སྐྱ་པའི།།
བསྟན་འཛིན་ཡོངས་ཀྱི་རལ་པའི་ཟུར་ཕུད་ལ།།
མཁས་དང་གྲུབ་པའི་ཞབས་སེན་ངལ་གསོ་བའི།།
ཁོ་བོའི་གཙུག་རྒྱན་སྟགས་འཚང་འདི་འདྲ་དཀོན།།

དེ་ནས་རྗེ་ལུང་ཏུ་ཞག་གཅིག་བསྡད། སང་ཉིན་དགེ་སྡིངས་ན་དཔལ་ས་སྐྱའི་ཆོས་ཀྱིས་མངོན་པར་མཐོ་བའི་ཁྲི་ལ་བཞུགས་པ། བདག་ཆེན་རིན་པོ་ཆེ་ཁྲི་ཐོག་པའི་དྲུང་བཞུགས་པ་དང་མཇལ། དེ་སྔ་ནས་དཔོན་སློབ་འདྲིས་པ་ལྷ་བུའི་ནང་གཙང་ཞིང་ཐུགས་འགོལ་བས་བཀའ་ལུང་བག་ཕེབས་པར་གནང་། དེད་རྣམས་ལ་བདག་ཆེན་ཐམས་ཅད་མཁྱེན་པ་ཆེན་

The nectar of the great
secret made my heart content.

O friends, don't fear
the color of the sea;
board the ship of faith!

By the kindness of the captain,
the excellent spiritual friend,
the jewels of attainment
will be found—have no doubt.

A mantra bearer such as
this crown ornament of mine,
an expert and realized being
whose toenails rest on the braided
topknots of all holders of the doctrine
of the venerable lords of Sakya,
is rare upon the surface of the earth.

Then we stayed for a day and night in Dzilung. The next day we met the current Dakchen Rinpoché, occupant of the lofty Dharma throne of glorious Sakya, who

པོས་མཛད་པའི་བླ་མ་མཆོད་ཆོག་རྒྱས་བསྡུས་ཀྱི་ལུང་། དེ་དང་རྗེས་སུ་འབྲེལ་བའི་བླ་མའི་རྣལ་འབྱོར་འདོད་ཞུས་ལྟར་བཀའ་དྲིན་བསྐྱངས།

སྐུ་ན་ཕྲ་མོ་དེ་ལྷ་བུ་ལ་འདི་འདྲའི་ལུགས་གཉིས་ཀྱི་གནང་སྐྱོང་དང་ངོ་མཚར་བ་འོང་བ་ངེས་པར་འཇམ་པའི་དབྱངས་ཀྱི་རྣམ་འཕྲུལ་ཡིན་པ་ལ་ཐེ་ཚོམ་མི་ཟ་བ་འདུག་སྙམ་པའི་དད་མོས་དང་། ས་སྐྱ་པའི་རྫོངས་ཞེན་གྱིས་བློ་བདེ་བ་ཚད་མེད་པ་བྱུང་། བྱིན་རླབས་ཀྱི་རྟེན་གནང་སྦྱིན་སོགས་ཡང་དག་ཐུགས་རྗེས་བཟུང་།

དེའི་ནུབ་ཁྲོ་ཕུར་ཕྱིན་འདུ་ཁང་ཆེན་པོ་ཞིག་འདུག་པ་དེར་སྡོད་ས་བྱས། ངེད་རང་གཅིག་པུར་ཞལ་རས་ལྷ་ཁང་གི་ཕྱི་སྐོར་བྱེད་ཅིང་ཡོད་ཙ་ན། སྐོར་ལམ་དེ་ན་བུད་མེད་གཞོན་ནུ་ནད་པ་ཡིན་ཟེར་བ་ཞིག་ཁྲིལ་བྱས་ནས་འདུག སྐོར་བ་འགའ་སོང་ཙ་ན་དེ་ལ་མཆེ་བ་ཇེ་རིང་ཇེ་རིང་ཡོང་གི་འདུག མིག་འཁྲུལ་བའམ། ཀུང་ཀུམ་ལྷ་བུ་ལ་བཙོས་ནས་འཇིགས་པ་སྟོན་པ་ཡིན་ནམ་སྙམ་པའི་ཚེ། མཐར་ཁ་ཐམས་ཅད་མཆེ་བ་སྐྱ་ཟང་ངེ་བ་མཐོ་རེ་ལྷག་པ་ཙམ་གྱིས་ཁེངས་པ། དཔྲལ་བའི་དཀྱིལ་ན་ཁྲག་གི་མིག་སྨན་ཚོ་ལུང་ཐང་གི་རྡོག་པོ་འདྲ་བ་ཞིག་བྱས་ཧར་ཏེ་ལངས་བྱུང་བས། འདི་སྲིན་མོའམ་འབབ་མོ་ལྷ་བུ་ཞིག་ཡིན་པ་འདུག་སྙམ།

ཡི་དམ་གྱི་ང་རྒྱལ་དང་བཅས་པས་ལག་ཏུ་ཕྲེང་བ་ཁྱེར་ནས་དེད་པས་སྐོར་ལམ་ལ་བྲོས་

was staying in Geding. He spoke at ease, intimately and leisurely, as if teacher and students were previously acquainted. According to my expressed wish, he favored us with the reading transmission of the extensive and condensed rites of offering to the masters, which the great omniscient Dakchen had composed, and the guruyoga connected to them.

Amazed that one so young was this capable in both traditions, I thought with faith and devotion that he was certainly, without doubt, an emanation of Mañjughoṣa. With the blind loyalty of a Sakya follower, measureless satisfaction arose. In his perfect compassion he graced us with blessed sacred objects, gifts, and so forth.

That evening we went to Tropu. We found a place to stay in the great assembly hall there. When I was alone doing outer circumambulations of the Face-Viewing Temple, a young woman who said she was sick was squatting on that circumambulation path. While I did several circumambulations, her fangs were growing longer and longer. As I thought, "Is it a hallucination or has she made something like fake fangs to frighten me?" finally her entire mouth was filled with bright white fangs, each more than a handspan long. A bloody eye about the size of the nut of a soapberry tree had formed in the center of her forehead. When she suddenly stood up, I thought, "This is some kind of demoness or witch."

With the pride of the chosen deity, I took my string of beads in hand and

སོང་། རྗེས་ལ་བཙུག་ཕྱིན་པས་ལྷོ་ཕྱོགས་ཀྱི་ཁྲིམ་ཚང་གི་ནང་ཞིག་ཏུ་བྲོས་ནས་སྒོ་དེ་ནང་ནས་བཙད་སོང་།

དེ་འཕྲལ་འོག་ཏུ་ཡོག་གམ་སླམ་པ་ལ། སེམས་ཐེང་བ་འདྲ་བ་ཞིག་བྱུང་ནས་སྐོར་བ་གསུམ་ཙམ་བྱས་པས། ཁང་པ་དེའི་སྟེང་ནས་བུད་མེད་དེའི་མགོ་འདྲ་བ་ཞིག་སྒྲ་ཟིང་ངེ་བ་མཐོང་ཙམ་བྱས། སྐད་གདངས་ངར་ཆེ་བའི་གདངས་མ་དབྱངས་ལ།

དད་མོས་ཀྱི་སྣང་བ་མི་འདུག་ཀྱང་།།
ཚེ་སྔོན་གྱི་ལས་འབྲེལ་གཅོད་ཐབས་མེད།།

ཁྲག་འཛག་སྲིན་པོའི་རི་ལ་འཕྲད།།
འཕན་དཀར་གྱི་ལྗོངས་སུ་རྗེས་སུ་འཛིན།།

འཛིགས་སྣང་ལོག་ལྟ་མ་བྱེད་ཨང་།།
བདེ་ཆེན་ལོངས་སྤྱོད་རྣལ་འབྱོར་པ།།

chased her. She fled along the circumambulation path. As I followed, she fled into a family home to the south and shut the door from inside.

Instantly I thought, "Should I go back?" But a sort of hesitation arose. When I had done about three circumambulations, on top of that house I caught a glimpse of tangled hair like that woman's head. In a voice with a very strong melody, she called out:

> You have no feeling
> of faith and devotion,
> but there's no way to cut
> the karmic link of past lives.
>
> On Bloody Mount Sinpo
> we'll meet.
>
> In the land of Penkar
> I'll grace you.
>
> Don't feel frightened;
> don't have the wrong view!
>
> Yogin, you'll enjoy ecstasy . . .

ཟེར་བ་ཞིག་ལབ་བྱུང་བའི་མོད་ལ་སྤྲར་གྱི་འཛིགས་སྣང་དེ་ཞིག་པ་འདྲ་བའི་རིག་པ་ཧད་དེ་ཚོད་དེ་བ། ལུས་ལྡིད་མེད་པ་འདྲ་བའི་ཟ་ཟི་བན་བུན། རྟོག་པ་གར་རྒྱབ་མི་ཤེས་པ། སྣང་བ་འདི་གསལ་ལ་གཏད་སོ་མེད་པ་སྐད་བརྟན་ལ་རྒྱུག་གམ་སྙམ་པ་ཞིག་བྱུང་བས་

འདི་བར་ཆད་དམ་དངོས་གྲུབ་གང་ཡིན་མི་ཤེས་པ་འདུག

ད་རེས་ནས་བརྡ་ཞིག་སྟོན་པ་མ་བྱུང་། ད་མངོན་དུ་མ་གྱུར་པ་ལ་གསང་དགོས་སྙམ་ཟླ་བོ་རྣམས་ལ་བསྒྲོས་ཡེ་མ་བཏང་།

དེའི་ནུབ་འོག་གི་འདུ་ཁང་ནང་གི་ཞྭོག་བུར་བསྡད་པའི་ཚེ། གཏོར་བཟློ་སོགས་སྒྲོས་བཅས་ཀྱི་དགེ་སྦྱོར་རྣམས་ཀྱང་དེ་གའི་ངང་དུ་འགྲོ་བ་ཞིག་བྱུང་། ཅི་ཡིན་ནམ་ཆ་མེད་ཡ་མཚན་ནི་ཆེ་སྙམ་དགེ་སྦྱོར་གྱི་ངང་དུ་སྲིལ། དེར་བྱམས་ཆེན། སྐུ་འབུམ་ཆེན་མོ། རྣམ་སྲས་རང་བྱོན་སོགས་མཇལ། ཕྱག་མཆོད་སྨོན་ལམ་ཡིད་ཆེས་པ་བཏབ།

སང་ཚ་ཐོན་ལ་དགེ་སྡིངས་ནས་བདག་ཆེན་རིན་པོ་ཆེའི་ཕྱག་ཕྱི་དྲུང་འཁོར་གཞོན་པ་ཁ་ཅིག་ཀྱང་གནས་མཇལ་ལ་བྱུང་། ངེད་ཚོས་ཇ་བཟང་པོ་བསྐོལ་ནས་དྲངས། དག་སྣང་བྱས་ཐམས་ཅད་བསྒོངས་ནས་ཞལ་རས་ལྷ་ཁང་མཇལ། དེ་ན་ཕག་མོ་ཞལ་གཉིས་མའི་སྐུ་ལི་མ་ཞིག་འདུག་པ་དེའི་ཕག་ཞལ་དང་ཐོག་གི་བར་ལ་ཤེལ་གྱི་འཁར་བ་བཙུགས་པ་ལྟ་བུ་ཞིག་འདུག་པས།

འདི་གང་ཡིན་བྱས་ལག་པ་རེག་པས་འོད་མ་གཏོགས་རེག་རྒྱུ་མི་འདུག

དཀོན་གཉེར་དེ་ན་རེ། དེ་ཕག་ཞལ་ཡིན་པ་གདའ་ཟེར།

As she spoke, a blank shock of pure awareness dawned, as if that previous feeling of fear had vanished. I felt shaky and ephemeral, like my body was weightless. I didn't know how to take a step. The thought arose, "This appearance is clear, but there's no point of reference. Should I scream and run?"

I couldn't tell if this were an obstacle or an attainment.

"Just now no sign has been shown," I thought. "Now it's not obvious and must be kept secret." I didn't discuss it at all with my companions.

That evening, while staying in a tent inside the lower assembly hall, even the elaborate practices such as the dedication of sacrificial cakes passed in just that

Tropu

དེ་ཁོང་རྣམས་ཀྱིས་མ་མཐོང་བ་འདུག་པས་ཁ་རོག་བསྡད། སྐུ་དེ་ལ་མགོ་གཏུགས་ཏེ་དབང་བཞི་བླངས་སྨོན་ལམ་བཏབ་བོ།

ལར་རྗེ་བཙུན་མཁའ་སྤྱོད་དབང་མོ་འདི་དེད་རང་ལ་ཐོག་མ་ནས་དགྱེས་པ་ཞིག་ཡིན་འདུག་པས། རྗེ་བཙུན་རྗོ་རིང་པ་ཆེན་པོའི་གསུང་ནས་ཀྱང་། ཆོས་རྗེ་ལ་མཁའ་སྤྱོད་མའི་བྱིན་རླབས་བྱུས་རེས་ཀྱི་དེད་ལ་ལྷུས་ཁྱད་པར་ཅན་རེ་ཡོང་གི་འདུག འབད་རྩོལ་མཛད་ན་འདིས་མཁའ་སྤྱོད་ལ་འཁྲིད་ཉེན་གདའོ་གསུང་བ་ཡོད་ཅིང་།

འདི་སྐོར་གྱི་གཏམ་མང་པོ་ཞིག་ཡོད་དེ། སྟོད་མི་འདུག་པས་ནམ་མཁའི་དབྱིངས་སུ་ཕཏ།

Nāro Khecarī

state. I wondered what it was, thinking it unique and marvelous, and sustained it within the practice. There I visited the great Maitreya, the great stūpa, the self-arisen Vaiśravaṇa, and so forth. I made prostrations, offerings, and prayers with conviction.

After mealtime the next day, several of Dakchen Rinpoché's young attendants and lay officials from Geding also came to visit the place. We brewed and served a fine tea. With deep appreciation, everyone joined together and visited the Face-Viewing Temple. A bronze alloy image of the two-faced Vārāhī was there. A crystal rod seemed to stretch between its sow face and the ceiling.

"What's this?" I asked, touching it with my hand. There was nothing to touch but light.

"That's the sow face," the steward replied.

They didn't see it. So I kept quiet. I touched my head to that image, took the four initiations, and made prayers.

In general, this venerable Queen of Khecara has been pleased with me from the beginning. The great venerable lord Doringpa had also said, "Exceptional omens appear to me every time I perform the blessing of Khecarī for the Dharma lord. If you make the effort, there's the risk she may lead you to Khecara."

I have a lot to say about this, but there's no worthy recipient. So into the expanse of space with it—*Phaṭ!*

སྤྲང་རྒྱལ་ཁམས་ཕྱོགས་མེད་རྒྱུ་བའི་ཚེ།།
ཡུལ་ཡ་མཚན་གྱི་ལྟད་མོ་འདི་ལྟར་མཐོང་།།

ཤབ་དགེ་སྡིངས་རྡོ་རྗེ་ཕོ་བྲང་ན།།
རྗེ་ས་སྐྱ་ལོ་ཙཱའི་སྐུ་ཡི་དགོན།།
ཐུགས་གཅིག་ཏུ་འདྲེས་པ་སྲས་ཀྱི་མཆོག།
ཁོང་འཛམ་དབྱངས་གཞོན་ནུ་དངོས་དང་མཇལ།།

གསུང་བག་ཡེབས་ཀྱི་བདུད་རྩི་སྙིང་ལ་སིམ།།
ཆོས་ཟབ་ལམ་གྱི་རྣལ་འབྱོར་བཀའ་དྲིན་ཞུས།།

ཁོང་སྐྱོན་བྲལ་གྱི་མཛད་འཕྲིན་མཐོང་བའི་ཚེ།།
ངེད་ས་སྐྱ་པའི་མདུན་མ་གྲུབ་འདུག་སྙམ།།

སེམས་དགའ་སྤྲོ་དང་དད་པས་མཆི་མ་འཁྲུག།
ཞབས་སྤྱི་གཙུག་ཏུ་བླངས་ནས་སྨོན་ལམ་བཏབ།།

A beggar, when aimlessly
roaming the country, saw the spectacle
of a marvelous place in this way.

In the vajra palace of Geding
at Shab, Lord Sakya Lotsā's nephew
and sublime spiritual son I met,
whose mind had blended as one with his.
He is youthful Mañjughoṣa for real.

The nectar of his casual
speech dissolved in my heart.
I requested as Dharma the favor
of the yoga of the profound path.

Seeing his flawless deeds
I thought, "The yearning of we
Sakya followers has been fulfilled."

With delight and faith I burst
into tears. Lifting his feet to the crown
of my head, I made prayers.

དེར་ཤབ་སྟོད་ཀྱི་ཆུ་ཀླུང་བརྒྱལ་ནས་ཕྱིན།།
ཡུལ་ཡ་མཚན་ཅན་ཁྲོ་ཕུའི་གཙུག་ལག་སླེབས།།

ལྷ་བྱམས་མགོན་གྱི་སྐུ་བརྙན་ཞལ་བཟང་མཐོང་།།
རྟེན་ཁྱད་པར་ཅན་ཀུན་ལ་བྱིན་རླབས་ཞུས།།

མ་མི་མིན་མཁའ་འགྲོས་འཛིགས་གཟུགས་བསྟན།།
ང་ཁྲོ་རྒྱལ་གྱི་ང་རྒྱལ་དབྱིངས་ནས་རྒྱས།།

མཚོན་འཕྲེང་ལྷུག་གིས་འདེད་དྲག་བཏང་བའི་ཚོ།།
ཁོང་ལུང་བསྟན་གྱི་སྒྲ་དབྱངས་སྒྲོག་པ་སྐད།།

ཁྲོད་ཡེ་ཤེས་ཀྱི་ཌཱ་ཀིའི་ལུང་བསྟན་དང་།།
མོ་ཤ་ཟན་གྱི་མཁའ་འགྲོའི་རྒྱུང་འདོད་གཉིས།།
ང་རྣལ་འབྱོར་གྱི་སེམས་ལ་བདེ་སྡུག་མེད།།
གང་ཡིན་ཡང་རང་ངོ་དབྱིངས་སུ་སླམ།།

Crossing the river there
in upper Shab, we traveled,
arriving at a marvelous
place, the temple of Tropu.

I saw the fine face of the image
of divine Maitreyanātha.
At all the exceptional sacred
objects, I requested blessings.

The mother ḍākinī who wasn't
human displayed a frightening form.
From basic space I expanded
with the pride of the Wrathful King.

When I fiercely chased her
with the whip of my string of beads
as a weapon, she proclaimed
a prophetic melody.

Both your prophecy of the ḍākinī
of primordial awareness and the cry
from afar of the flesh-eating ḍākinī,
neither please nor pain my yogin's mind.

ཨ་ལ་ལ་རྒྱལ་ཁམས་སྐོར་བའི་ཚོ།།
སྟོན་མེད་ཀྱི་ལྷད་མོ་ཨ་རེ་འཛིགས།།

སེམས་ཉིད་ཀྱི་རང་གདངས་ཡིན་པར་གོ།
དྲིན་ཅན་གྱི་བླ་མ་དེ་སྐུ་དྲིན་ཆེ།།

དཔལ་མཁའ་སྤྱོད་ཀྱི་དགའ་མ་ཡིད་འོང་མ།།
དུས་རིང་ནས་བསྐྱངས་པའི་མ་མ་དེས།།
ད་རིག་འཛིན་གྱི་གྲུབ་པ་སྟེར་བའི་བརྡ།།
ཡོངས་ཛོ་མཚར་གྱི་གློས་གར་ཅི་ཡང་རྩེ།།

The very essence of either
is equal in basic space.

A La La! While touring
the country, a spectacle
so frightening, as never before:

I understood it was the natural
radiance of the essence of mind.
That kind master was so very kind.

The lovely beauty from glorious
Khecara, that nanny who's cared
for me for so long, as a sign of now
giving an awareness holder's attainment,
displayed all sorts of wondrous drama.

དེ་ནས་གནས་ཀྱི་མདའ་ན་དམ་པ་དམར་པོའི་རུས་ཡིན་ཟེར་བ་ཞིག་གི་ལག་ན་དམ་པའི་གདུང་རུས་ལས་གྲུབ་པའི་སྤྱན་རས་གཟིགས་ཀྱི་སྐུ་དང་སྲུས་ཀྱི་ཕྱུགས་རང་བྱོན་ཡིན་ཟེར་བ་སོགས་འདུག་པ་མཇལ།

དེའི་ནུབ་གངས་ཅན་ཆོས་འཕེལ་གྱི་དགོན་པའི་འཁྲིས། ལྷ་མོ་དམག་ཟོར་མའི་བླ་མཚོ་ཡིན་ཟེར་བ། མཐའ་སྐོར་པའི་ཚུལ་གྱིས་བསྐོར་བའི་དབུས་ན་ནེའུ་གསེང་གི་དཀྱིལ་ན་མཚོ་ཆུང་ཁོར་ར་ཞིག་འདུག་པའི་ཁ་སྟོད་སྐྱིད་སྐྱིད་འདྲ་བ་ཞིག་འདུག་པ་དེར་ལྟོག་གྲུ་བྱས་བསྡད། ཇ་བཟང་བསྐོལ་ཞིང་ཆོས་སྤྱོད་བྱས་པས་གྲུ་པ་རྣམས་བྱོན་བྱུང་ནས།

འདི་པ་ཆ་ལུགས་སོགས་རྟོགས་ལྡན་དུ་མི་འདུག གྲུ་མཐུན་ལ་སྐྱིད་མདོག་རྣམ་པ་སྔོ་ཡངས་པ་ཞིག་འདུག་པས། སྡེ་པ་ཟིལ་གནོན་པ་ལྟ་བུ་ཞིག་བརྫུས་པ་ཡིན་ནམ་ཟེར།

གཅིག་ན་རེ་ང་དང་ཞལ་འདྲིས་ཡོད། སྡེ་པ་ཟིལ་གནོན་པ་ཡིན་ཐག་ཆོད་འདུག་ཟེར་བས། ཕལ་ཆེར་དེ་ལ་ཡིད་ཆེས་སོང་། སུ་ཡིན་ཟེར་བ་ལ།

ང་ཅི་མེད་ཀྱི་སྤྲང་པོ་ཡན་པ་བློ་བདེ་བྱ་བ་ཡིན་ནོ་ཨང་བྱས་པས།

ཁྱེད་རང་སུ་ཡིན་ཡང་ཉམས་དགའ་ལ་སྣང་བ་བདེ་བ་ཞིག་འདུག་ཟེར་རོ།

ཐག་ཁྲ་སྦྲུལ་དུ་འཁྲུལ་པའི་སྣང་ངོ་ན།།
འཇིགས་སྐྲག་འཁྲོས་ལ་ཕྱུག་པ་དོན་བྱེད་ནུས།།

ཡིད་ཆེས་མོས་གུས་ལྡན་པའི་གང་ཟག་ལ།།
ཁྱི་སོ་རིང་བསྲེལ་ཕུང་པོར་སོང་ངོ་སྐད།།

Then, in the lower valley of the place, we visited such sacred objects as an Avalokiteśvara image said to have been created from Dampa's bone, and the self-arisen heart of his son, which were in the hands of a man said to be a descendent of Dampa Marpo.

That night, near Gangchen Chöpel Monastery, in the center of a meadow surrounded by groves of trees at the edges, there was a little lake with a camping place, said to be the spirit lake of the goddess Maksorma. We pitched the tents and stayed there on its enchanting upper shores. When we had brewed a fine tea and performed the Dharma liturgy, some monks came.

"This one's dress and so on aren't those of a realized yogin," they said. "Monk, you're a friendly person, pleasant and easygoing. Are you someone like the ruler Silnönpa in disguise?"

"I know you," one said. "You're definitely the ruler Silnönpa." Most of them believed him, but they asked, "Who are you?"

"I'm a poor beggar called Carefree Vagabond!" I replied.

"Whoever you are," they said, "you're a delightfully cheerful person."

In mistaken perception
of a rope as a snake,
terror can make you flee.

For a person with belief
and devotion, it's said,
the tooth of a dog
became a heap of relics.

མིང་ཙམ་བརྡ་ཙམ་བཏགས་པ་ཕོ་ན་ལའང་།།
རང་རང་ངོ་བོས་གྲུབ་པ་རྡུལ་ཙམ་མེད།།

ཅི་མེད་ཅིར་ཡང་འཆར་བའི་ངོ་མཚར་ཅན།།
རྟེན་འབྲེལ་ཟབ་མོའི་རང་མཚང་དེ་ཏུ་རིག།

སྐྱེ་བོས་བཞི་མདོར་སྨྲ་བའི་ཁུངས་མེད་གཏམ།།
གང་ཟེར་བདེན་པར་འཛིན་པའི་བློ་ཆུང་ཚོས།།
གཞི་མེད་རི་བོང་ཅལ་གྱི་སྒྲ་དབྱངས་ཀྱིས།།
རང་གཞན་མང་པོའི་རང་མཚང་སྟོན་ཉེན་གདའ།།

Chumik

In what's only
been given just a name,
just a label, not even
an atom is established
by own-essence.

The nature of amazing,
profound interdependence,
nothing appearing as anything,
is realized there.

Small-minded persons,
who accept as true
the baseless gossip
people speak at crossroads,
risk revealing their own
and many other people's faults
with a song of groundless,
nervous alarm.

སྟག་ལ་སྐྱ་མོ་དུང་གི་སྒོ་བཀལ་ཏེ། རྗེ་བཙུན་ས་སྐྱ་པའི་གདུང་བརྒྱུད་རིམ་པས་བྱིན་གྱིས་བརླབས་པའི་གནས་གཙང་ཆུ་མིག་རིང་མོར་སླེབས། དེ་ནུབ་གནས་འབྲེལ་བྱས། སྟོན་ཟངས་དཀར་ལོ་ཙཱ་བས་བཞེངས་པའི་གཙུག་ལག་ཁང་། གཉན་སྒྲོལ། འཕགས་པ་རིན་པོ་ཆེའི་སྐུ་འདྲ་སོགས་བཞུགས་པའི་ལྷ་ཁང་། བདག་ཆེན་རིན་པོ་ཆེ་གྲགས་བློ་པས་བཞེངས་པའི་མགོན་ཁང་སོགས་མཇལ། གསོལ་གདབ་སྨོན་ལམ་ཡིད་ཆེས་པར་བྱས།

དེ་དག་ལ་ངོ་མཚར་ཞིང་བྱིན་རླབས་ཀྱི་ཟིལ་གཞན་དང་མི་འདྲ་བ་ཞིག་འདུག་པས་དད་མོས་ཚད་མེད་པ་སྐྱེས། དིང་སང་ཞབས་ཏོག་བདག་རྐྱེན་ཆེར་མེད་པའི་གོགས་ཉམས་ཆེན་པོ་འདུག་པ་ལ་སེམས་ཀྱིས་མི་བཟོད་པའི་སྐྱོ་སྣང་ཡང་ཡོད་པ་ཞིག་བྱུང་།

སང་ཉིན་ཉི་མ་ཕྱེད་ཡོལ་ཙམ་ན་ངོར་ཨེ་ཝཾ་ཆོས་ལྡན་དུ་སླེབས། མཇོ་མོ་ར་བ་ཡོད་པའི་སྤང་སྟེང་དེར་ཚོག་སྒར་བྱས་བསྡད། ལམ་ཟབ་ལྷ་ཁང་དུ་བླ་མའི་རྣལ་འབྱོར་རྒྱས་པ་ཞིག་བླངས། སྤྱི་སྨོས་ཀྱི་བསྟན་པ་རྒྱས་པའི་སྨོན་ལམ་བཏབ། གཞན་ཡང་ལམ་འབྲས་ལྷ་ཁང་གིས་གཙོ་བྱས་པའི་རྟེན་གསུམ་རྣམས་ཀྱང་མཇལ། དཔོན་པོ་རིན་ཆེན་སེང་གེ་བས་གཞིས་ལེན་སྐབས་བབ་བྱས། ཁྲིམ་ཐོག་དཔོན་པོ་སོགས་འདོད་ཆོས་དགོས་ཟེར་བ་མང་དག་བྱུང་བས། ཐོག་ཙིག་ལ་གུར་མགོན་གྱི་རྗེས་གནང་བྱས། འཕྲལ་མཁོའི་ཇ་གོས་དར་སོགས་འབུལ་བའང་འགའ་བྱུང་།

Crossing Tak Pass, the gate to Kyamodung, we arrived at Chumik Ringmo in Tsang, a place the hereditary lineage of the venerable lords of Sakya has successively blessed. That evening we established a connection with the place. We visited the temple that Sangkar Lotsāwa first built; the temple containing the Tārā of Nyan, an image of Pakpa Rinpoché, and so on; the temple of the protectors that Dakchen Rinpoché Draklopa built; and so forth. We made supplications and prayers with conviction.

Those had a marvelous and blessed aura unlike others, so boundless faith and devotion arose. Nowadays they are in great disrepair, without much service and care, so I also had an unbearable feeling of sadness.

Just past noon the next day we arrived at Ngor Ewam Chöden. We pitched our tent camp and stayed there in a pasture fenced in for hybrid yak cows. I practiced an extensive guruyoga in the Profound Path Temple and made prayers for the expansion of the general and specific doctrine. Furthermore, I also visited the three types of sacred objects, with those in the Temple of the Path with the Result foremost. The nephew Rinchen Sengé gave us a timely welcome. When prominent nephews and so forth came, many saying they had to have Dharma teachings they desired, I gave the ritual permission of Pañjaranātha on a rooftop. I also received some offerings of immediate necessities such as tea, clothing, and silk scarves.

དེ་ནས་ཞ་ལུ་ལ་ཆས་ཏེ་ཕྱིན་པའི་ལམ་བར་ནས་ལྷུགས་སྟོད་མཐོང་བྱུང་བས། ངེད་ཚོ་ས་སྐྱ་པའི་ཡུས་པོ་ཆེའི་མི་གསུམ་གྱི་ནང་ནས། ཤར་སྨད་བཙོང་ཁའི་དགེ་བཤེས་རིན་ཆེན་བརྩོན་འགྲུས་ཀྱི་བརྒྱུད་པ། དཔོན་ཆེན་དབེན་ཤྲཱི་རྒྱལ་བ་བཟང་པོ་དང་། ཏུ་ཤྲཱི་རྒོད་པོ་རིན་ཆེན་སོགས་རིམ་པར་བརྒྱུད་པའི་ཕ་ཚན་ཤིན་ཏུ་ཉེ་བ་ཞིག་ཡིན་པས། ཁོང་ཚོ་དར་རྒྱུད་དང་བདེ་དོག་གང་འདྲ་ཞིག་ཡོད་དམ་སྙམ་དགོས་མེད་འཛིག་རྟེན་གྱི་རྗོངས་ཞེན་ཞིག་སྐྱེས།

ཞུ་རག་གི་བསམ་པ་མེད་ཀྱང་བྱ་བྲལ་གྱི་གནས་སྐབས་སེམས་ལ་གང་ཤར་ལག་ཏུ་བླངས་ཆོག་སྙམ་པས་དེར་ཕྱིན།

ཁོང་ཚོའི་གཞིས་ཀའི་སྟོད་དེར་ཞོག་གྲྭ་བྱས། ངས་ཞོག་ཕྱུར་བསྟད། ཁོང་གྲྭ་པ་རྣམས་ཉམས་དགའ་དང་སྤྲགས་པས་བསྔོ་བ་སྨོན་ལམ་བརྒྱབ་པས་མང་ཇ་ཟུང་ཇ་གདན་སྟོན་དང་བཅས་པ་བསྐྱལ་སོང་། སུ་ཡིན་ཟེར་བ་ལ་ངེད་རྣམས་ལ་སྟོད་མཐོན་པོ་ནས་ཡིན་ཟེར་བ་བྱས་ནའང་།

རྗེས་སུ་ངོར་པའི་གྲྭ་པ་འགའ་སོགས་རིམ་པར་བརྒྱུད་ནས་ཆ་ཙམ་ངོ་ཤེས་འདུག་པས། དཔོན་འོག་མ་འདྲ་བའི་མི་གཞོན་ཞིག་ངའི་རྩར་བྱུང་། འདི་འདྲ་ཡིན་པ་འདྲ་ཟེར་བའི་རྩད་གཅོད་ཞིབ་པོ་བྱེད་ཀྱིན་འདུག་པས་

ད་ཅི་ནས་ངེད་བྱ་བྲལ་དུ་སོང་བས་སྐུག་བྲོ་བྱས་དོགས་སྤྲུམ་མི་བསྟད་པ་ཡིན། ངོ་བོ་དེ་ལྟར་ཡིན་པས་མཇལ་འཕྲད་ཙམ་མཇད་འདོད་ཡོད་ན་དེ་ག་བགྱིས་པས་ཆོག་བྱས་པས་

ཁོ་ལོག་སོང་། རེ་ཞིག་ནས་སླེབས་ནས། དེང་སང་སྐུ་མཚམས་མེ་བ་ཞིག་ཡོད་པས་མཇལ་སྐབས་མ་བདེ་བྱུང་། སང་ཉིན་ཅིས་ཀྱང་བཞུགས་པ་གནང་དགོས་ཟེར་བ་ལ།

Ngor Monastery

Then we set out for Shalu and saw Chaktö from along the path as we traveled. Of the three men we Sakya followers are so boastful about, the lineage of the spiritual friend Rinchen Tsöndrü of Tsongkha in the east is that of my extremely close paternal relatives, in whose line Grand Governor Enshrī Gyalwa Sangpo, Hushrī Göpo Rinchen, and so on successively appeared. I thought, "What sort of ups and downs and happiness and suffering are they having?" A needless, mundane, blind loyalty arose.

I had no vague intention of asking but thought that as a mendicant it was acceptable to act on whatever dawned in the mind. So we went there.

མཇལ་བཞིན་མེད་པ་ཐུགས་དང་བསྟུན་པས་ཆོག་པ་འདུག ངེད་ཚོ་རྒྱལ་ཁམས་རིང་པོ་ཡོད་སྡོད་པའི་ལོང་མེད་བྱུས། དོན་ལ་རང་གི་རིགས་རུས་དང་ཕ་ཚན་སོགས་གང་ཡིན་གྱི་བླང་དོར་མེད་པའམ། ཡང་ན་མི་སྨུན་དུ་ངོ་འདྲིགས་མི་ཐུབ་པ་ཞིག་ཡོད་པ་ཡིན་ཡོང་། ང་ལ་ཤཱཀྱ་ཐུབ་པའི་བཀའ་དྲིན་གྱིས་ཕྱོགས་གང་ལ་ཕྱིན་ཡང་བསྙེན་བཀུར་བྱེད་མཁན་ནི་ཐོགས་མེད་འོང་གི་འདུག འདི་སྐོར་གྱི་ཞིབ་ཐག་དེ་ཆོད་པས་བློ་བདེ། ལར་བཙུན་པ་གཉེན་སྲིད་ཆེས་པ་ལ་དེ་འདྲ་མང་པོ་འཕྱོན། ཁྱོད་སྙིང་ཆོམ་ཆོམ་སྐྱམ་པ་བྱུས།

ནམ་ཟྲི་ལ་ལངས་ཕྱིན། ངེད་ཚོའི་རྗེས་ལ་ཆས་ཀ་ཕྲན་བུ་དང་བཅས་ལམ་སྣ་བ་ཡིན་ཟེར་བ་ཞིག་བཏང་བྱུང་།

མི་དགོས་ལོག་རྒྱུག་བྱས་ཀྱང་མི་ཉན་པར་ཞ་ལུ་བར་ཕྱིན།

Shalu Monastery

We pitched our tents there in the upper part of their estate. I stayed in a little tent. When the monks cheerfully performed dedication prayers, small offerings of tea were delivered, along with extra cushions. Asked who we were, they said, "We're from way up in Latö."

But later, several Ngor monks and so on gradually passed through and partially recognized us. So a young man who was like a lower official came up to me. He was inquiring in detail, saying, "It seems to be like this . . . ."

I said, "Now, in any case, I've become a mendicant. Afraid of repulsing you, we've camped appropriately. That's essentially how things stand. If [the governor] wishes to meet briefly, it's fine to do just that."

He went back. After a while he returned and said, "He's in a strict retreat these days, so it's not convenient to meet. You must surely stay tomorrow."

"That he feels no wish to meet is just fine," I said. "We don't have time to stay long in the countryside. Really, I'll either become free of acceptance and rejection of who my family line, paternal relatives, and so on are, or else I'll become one who can't be flattered in front of people. By the kindness of Śākyamuni, wherever I go people continually come to offer hospitality. I've decisively eliminated attachment about this, so I'm carefree. In general, monks have great attachment to their relatives, and many such will come. Think of what will satisfy your hearts."

At early dawn we got up and left. A man who said he was a guide was sent after us with a few provisions.

"We don't need you," I said. "Go back."

But he didn't listen and went as far as Shalu.

དེ་ནུབ་རྒྱན་གོང་གི་གཙུག་ལག་ཁང་གི་མགོན་ཁང་མཇལ་བས་དེར་གཏོར་མའི་འཁྲིས་སུ་བུད་མེད་གོས་དཀར་ཁྲ་གྱོན་པ་ཞིག་བྱུང་བ་དེ་མཐར་ཕྱི་ནང་གང་དུ་སོང་ཆ་མེད་པ་ལ་ཡལ་བ་ལྟ་བུ་ཞིག་བྱུང་། ཞ་ལུ་གནས་ཀྱི་གསེར་ཁང་གི་ཐུགས་རྗེ་ཆེན་པོས་གཙོ་བྱས་སྟེང་ཤོད་ཀྱི་ལྷ་ཁང་མགོན་ཁང་རྣམས་ཞིབ་པར་མཇལ།

གཞལ་ཡས་ཁང་གི་མདོ་དེར་དྲུང་ཆེན་བྱ་བ་ཡིན་ཟེར་བའི་གྱོང་རྒན་བཀའ་བརྒྱུད་པ་ལ་རྒྱབ་རྟེན་བཙོལ་བ། དོམ་ར་དང་སླིལ་བེམ་གྱི་སྒྲིབ་ཤིང་གྱོན་པ་ཞིག་དང་། དྲུང་རྒྱལ་བ་ཟེར་བའི་བན་གཞོན་མིག་ལྷག་པ་ན་ཡོད་པ་འདྲ་བ་ཞིག་འདུག་པས། ཁོང་ཚོས་ཇ་འདྲེན་གཞིས་ལེན་བྱས། ཁོང་རང་ཚོ་དང་བློ་བསྟུན་པའི་ཆ་ལེ་ཚོ་ལེ་མང་པོ་ལབས་བཏང་བས་ཤིན་ཏུ་དགའ་སོང་།

དེ་ན་རྗེ་ལས་པ་བྱ་བ་འགྲུལ་པ་ཐམས་ཅད་ལ་ཟ་འདོད་བྱེད་པ་ཞིག་འདུག་པས། སློང་མོ་དགོས་ཟེར་བྱུང་བས།

ངེད་རང་རྣམས་སྤྲང་པོ་ནི་མཉམ་པོར་འདུག ཁྱེད་ཚོ་ཞ་ལུ་པ་ཡིན་སྙམ་པ་ཡོད་ནའང་།
ངེད་ཚོ་འདར་པ་ཡིན་སྤྲད་ཚོག་བྱས་པས་

ཐམས་ཅད་བཞད་གད་ཐེག་གེ་བྱུང་ནས་ཟ་འདོད་ཆེར་མ་བྱས།

དེ་ནུབ་རི་ཕུག་ཏུ་ཕྱིན། བུ་སྟོན་ཐམས་ཅད་མཁྱེན་པའི་ཆོས་ཁྲིའི་མདུན་དེར་ཕྱོག་གྲྭ་བྱས་བཤད། ནཱ་ལེནྡྲའི་བཅོ་བརྒྱད་པའི་འཚོ་བྱེད་ཅིག་ཡོད་པ་དེས་གཞིས་ལེན་བསྙེན་བཀུར་ཟུར་ཆས་སོགས་ཞབས་ཏོག་ཡང་དག་བྱས།

That night, when I visited the chapel of the protectors in the Gyengong Temple, a woman wearing a white gown with multicolored designs appeared there beside the sacrificial cakes. Finally, without having gone anywhere outside or inside, she seemed to vanish. I carefully visited the upper and lower temples and the chapels of the protectors, with the Mahākaruṇika of the Serkhang at the site of Shalu foremost.

In that lower valley of the temple there was a grouchy old man who said he was called Drungchen and trusted in the Kagyü tradition as his support. He had a bearskin visor and wore concealment wood on his yak-hair robe. And there was a young monk called Drung Gyalwa, whose eyes seemed to be in his temples. They served tea and welcomed us. When I spoke a lot of nonsense agreeable to them, they were very pleased.

A man there called Jolepa, who acted greedy toward all travelers, said, "I need alms."

"We beggars are all equal," I said. "I think you're all from Shalu, but you can still give to us who are from Dar."

Everyone laughed and tittered, and he no longer acted so greedy.

That evening we went to Ripuk. We pitched our tents and stayed there in front of the Dharma throne of the omniscient Butön. A physician of the Nālendra Chogyé abbot was there who served us perfectly, greeting us with hospitality, special gifts, and so forth.

སང་དེ་རི་ཕུག་བླ་བྲང་ན་བཞུགས་པའི་བུ་སྟོན་རིན་པོ་ཆེའི་སྐུ་འདྲ་ཕྱག་ནས་མས་གཙོ་བྱས་པའི་རྟེན་གསུམ་ཤར་ཆེན་གྱི་རྟེན་སོགས་ཞིབ་པར་མཇལ།

མཁྱེན་རབ་རིན་པོ་ཆེའི་ཞལ་སློབ་བགྲེས་པོ་ཞིག་འདུག་པ་ལ་ཕྱག་རྫོར་འགྲོ་བཟང་གི་དབང་། རྣམ་སྲས་ཞི་དྲག་གི་རྗེས་གནང་། རྡོ་རྗེ་རབ་བརྟན་མའི་བཀའ་གཏད་ཡིག་ལུང་དང་བཅས་པ་ཞུས།

དེ་ནུབ་རྫིང་ཕུར་བྲག་སྐོ་བ་ཟེར་བའི་ཁམས་པ་ཕྱུག་པོ་ཞིག་གིས་གདན་དྲངས་དེར་ཕྱིན། ཚེ་དབང་། རྟ་མགྲིན་གྱི་རྗེས་གནང་སོགས་བྱས། ཇ་བཟང་པོ་ཞིག་ཕུལ་བྱུང་བས་ལམ་ཇ་ལ་ཤིན་ཏུ་མཁོ་བ་བྱུང་།

Ripuk

The next day I carefully visited the three types of sacred objects kept in the Ripuk monastic residence (of which the image of Butön Rinpoché that had been consecrated with barley from his own hand was foremost), the reliquary of Sharchen, and so forth.

There was an elderly personal disciple of Khyenrab Rinpoché from whom I requested the initiation of Vajrapāṇi in the tradition of Sugati, the ritual permissions of the calm and the wrathful Vaiśravaṇa, and the bestowal of authority for Dorjé Rabtenma, together with the reading transmission of the texts.

That evening a rich man from Kham called Drakgowa invited me to Dzingpu. I went there and performed a longevity initiation, the ritual permission of Hayagrīva, and so forth. He offered a fine tea, so we had tea for the road, which is crucial.

ཞེན་མེད་ཀྱི་ཉེ་དུའི་སྐོ་བསྐྱེགས་པས།།
དགོས་མེད་ཀྱི་ལམ་སྟོབས་དེ་ཏུ་བཅག།

དོན་མེད་ཀྱི་ལུང་སྡུག་བསྐོར་བའི་འབྲས།།
འབྲེལ་མེད་ཀྱི་ས་མཚམས་དེ་ཏུ་བྲིས།།

སྤྱིར་སེམས་ཅན་ཀུན་དྲིན་ཅན་ཕ་མར་འདུག།
སྒོས་སུ་བྱམས་གཉེན་ལ་གང་སྐྱིད་ཡུལ།།
ང་བྱ་བྲལ་གྱི་འདུན་མ་ཡང་རྩེར་ཡོད།།
ཁྱེད་ཕ་ཚན་སྐུ་ཁམས་ཅི་བདེར་བཞུགས།།

དཔལ་ཞ་ལུ་གསེར་ཁང་གི་དགོན་པ་ན།།
བན་སྐྱོན་ཀུན་གྱི་རིང་ཤལ་འཛུགས་བྱེད།།

མི་བསད་ལ་ཡ་ཕུད་མི་གདའ་བས།།
སྤྲང་པོ་ངས་རི་ཕུག་དགོན་པར་བྲོས།།

སྤྱར་འདྲིས་ཀྱི་སློབ་མས་ཞབས་ཏོག་བཟང་།།

Arriving desireless
at the door of kinfolk,
the needless compulsion
of the path was there broken.

The result of worthless
touring of valley interiors
was seeing pointless boundaries
had there been drawn.

In general, all sentient beings
have been our kind parents.
In particular, so have loving
relatives. For all of you to be
where you will be happy
is my highest aim as a mendicant.

You paternal relatives—
stay always in good health.

In Serkhang Monastery
of glorious Shalu,
all the crazy monks
stab with swords.

ཀུ་སུ་ལུའི་བླ་མ་ལམ་དུ་མཇལ།།
གང་ཞུས་ཀྱི་ཆོས་འབྲེལ་ལྷུག་པར་གནང་།།
ཁོང་བཀའ་དྲིན་མི་ཆུང་ཆེ་བར་འཁུམས།།

ལར་ད་ལྟ་གངས་རིའི་ལྗོངས་འདི་ན།།
དགོན་སྡེ་ཆོས་ཀྱི་རང་ཚུགས་འཛིན་པ་ལ།།
ཁོང་འགྲུན་ཟླ་བྲལ་བའི་ཞ་ལུ་པ།།
བོད་ཆོས་སྡེ་ཚོའི་སྲོག་ཤིང་དམ་པ་ལགས།།

ཁོང་བྲག་སྐོ་བ་བྱ་བའི་ཕྱུག་པོ་དེ།།
མིག་རྒྱ་ཁབ་ལས་ཕྲ་བ་ཞིག་ཡིན་ཟེར་ནའང་།།
ང་བྱ་བྲལ་ལ་ལམ་ཇ་བཟང་པོ་ཕུལ།།
དུས་གཞན་གྱི་ཇ་སིགས་གཅིག་ལས་དགའ།།

ཁོས་ཁེངས་དྲེགས་ཀྱིས་བརྙས་པ་ཡིན་ལས་ཆེ།།
ཡུལ་རྒྱན་གོང་གི་ལྷ་མོ་དེ་གནོད་ཀྱི་འདུག།

They don't shrink
from killing people,
so I, a beggar, fled
to Ripuk Monastery.

A disciple of previous
acquaintance offered fine service.

On the path I met
a mendicant master.

What Dharma connections
I requested, he freely granted.

His kindness was not
small but great, I know.

Generally, now in this
land of glacial mountains,
most monasteries adhere
independently to Dharma.

But those followers
of matchless Shalu

ངས་གཏོར་མ་དང་བཀའ་བསྒོ་དྲག་པོ་བྱས།།
དེ་རེ་ཞིག་ཡོག་ནས་བདེ་བར་བྱུང་།།

Panam Fortress

are the excellent backbone
of abbeys in Tibet.

That rich man called
Drakgowa was said to have
an eye finer than that of a needle.

But to me, a mendicant,
he offered fine tea for the road.

I was more pleased than
by a brick of tea at another time.

Most probably offended
by his arrogance,
the goddess of the Gyengong
region was hurting him.

I offered sacrificial cakes
and gave harsh commands.

After a while she retreated,
and he became comfortable.

དེ་ནས་ཐར་པ་དགོན་པར་སླེབས། དེ་ཉུབ་བསྡད་ནས་དེའི་སྟེང་ཤོད་ཀྱི་ལྷ་ཁང་མགོན་ཁང་རྣམས་ཞིབ་པར་མཇལ།

སང་ཚེ་ཐོག་ཏུ་སྨན་ལུང་དུ་ཕྱིན། ཕྲ་བྲང་པ་དེ་པ་དང་གཉེན་ཚན་རྙིང་པ་ཞིག་ཏུ་འགྲོ་བས་ངོ་ཤེས་བྱས། གཞིས་ལེན་ཡང་དག་བྱུང་། ནཱ་རོའི་རྒྱན་དྲུག་ཁ་ཆེ་པཎ་ཆེན་གྱི་སྐུ་ཆོས་སོགས་ཀྱི་བྱིན་རླབས་ཞུས། གཙང་ཁང་གི་རྟེན་གསུམ། སྒྲི་ཧྲིའི་གདུང་འབུམ་སོགས་མཇལ། སྟག་ཞོན་མགོན་ཁང་དུ་གཏོར་གསོལ་སྨན་དར་འཕྲིན་བཅོལ་ཡིད་ཆེས་པར་བྱས།

དེ་ནས་པ་རྣམ་གཞུང་ལ་ཕྱིན། ཕྲོང་སྟོད་དུ་ཞག་སྡོད་བྱས། སང་ཉིན་སྔ་བར་ཕྱིན་ལྷུན་གྲུབ་རྩེར་སླེབས། ངས་གནས་ཚང་ཞིག་ཏུ་བསྡད། ཟླ་བོ་རྣམས་གཟིམས་ཁང་སོགས་ཀྱི་ལྟད་མོ་དང་། ཞར་ལ་བསོད་སྙོམས་ཀྱང་བྱེད། སྡེ་དཔོན་ཆོས་ལ་དགའ་པོ་ཞིག་ཡོད་པ་ལ་འདུག་ཟེར་ནས་སོང་། ཁོང་རྣམས་ཀྱིས་ཉི་ཕྱེད་བར་བསྒུགས་པས་ལན་ཙམ་ཡང་མ་ཁུགས། ངེད་རང་རྣམས་ཀྱི་ཚ་ཐེབས་ཀྱང་ཆག་པ་ཞིག་བྱུང་ནས་ལོག་བྱུང་།

ལར་གནངས་ཆུང་ལ་བློ་རིག་ཆོད་པའི་སྡེ་དཔོན་དཔོན་སྐྱའི་རིགས་འདི། ལུག་ཐུག་གི་སྒྲོ་བས་ཕ་མོའི་ཉིན་ཐེབས་གཅིག་པ་མ་གཏོགས་དགོས་པ་མི་འདུག་པས་དེ་འདྲའི་རིགས་ལ་བྱ་བྲལ་རྣམས་ལམ་གཞུང་སྐྱོང་བ་རང་གནད་དུ་གདའ།

Then we arrived at Tarpa Monastery. We stayed that night, and I carefully visited its upper and lower temples and the chapels of the protectors.

At mealtime the next day we went to Menlung. My family ties with that occupant of the monastic residence go way back, so I recognized him. We received a perfect welcome. I requested the blessing of the six ornaments of Nāropa, the Dharma robe of the great paṇḍita of Kashmir, and so forth. I visited the three types of sacred objects in the sanctuary, the reliquary stūpa of Smṛti, and so on. I refreshed the sacrificial cakes in the protector chapel of Takshön, offered ceremonial scarves, and invoked his actions with conviction.

Then we traveled into the center of Panam and stayed for a day and night in the upper part of the village. We left early the next day and arrived at Lhundrup Tsé. I stayed at an inn. My companions went to see sights such as the official residence and also begged for alms along the way. It was said there was a ruling chieftain sympathetic to the Dharma, so they went. They waited until midday but didn't even get so much as a reply. After even our reason to hope for food was destroyed, they came back.

In general, this type of ruling chieftain (a lay chieftain clever in trivial matters) is of no use except as a pack ram's leather bag that dashes a fox's daylong hopes. With such types, it's crucial for mendicants to just keep going straight down the middle of the road.

དེ་ནས་བསམ་སྡིངས་དགོན་པར་སླེབས་ནས་དེ་ཉུབ་གནས་འབྲེལ་བྱས་བསྡད། སང་ཉིན་དེའི་ནི་གུ་བརྒྱད་པའི་ཕོ་ཁྲིམ་མགོན་ཁང་། ཡང་དགོན་གྱི་ལྷ་ཁང་མགོན་ཁང་སོགས་མཇལ། ཆོས་རྗེའི་དྲུང་དུ་ངེད་དཔོན་སློབ་རྣམས་ཀྱིས་བླ་མའི་རྣལ་འབྱོར་གྱི་ཆོས་འབྲེལ་ཞུས། སྐེར་གྱིས་མགོན་དཀར་གྱི་རྗེས་གནང་ཞུས་པས་མ་གནང་བར། རྩིས་ཀྱི་མགོན་པོ་ལྷ་ཆེན་དཔལ་འབར་གྱི་རྗེས་གནང་བཀའ་དྲིན་བསྐྱངས།

དེ་ནས་རྩིས་གནས་གསར་གྱི་ལྷ་ཁང་མགོན་ཁང་རྣམས་མཇལ། སྡེ་པ་བསོད་ནམས་རབ་བརྟན་པས་གཞིས་ལེན་ཤངས་ལེན་སོགས་ཡང་དག་མཛད། དེར་འདོལ་ཆུང་ན་ཚ་མོ་ཞིག་ཡོད་པ་དེས་འཕོད་དུ་རྟ་པ་གཉིས་རྐང་ཚུགས་བཏང་བྱུང་ནས་ཅིས་ཀྱང་ཡོང་དགོས་པའི་ནན་ཏན་བྱེད་ཀྱི་འདུག་པས་ཁོང་བྱིངས་པོ་དེར་བཞག ངེད་དཔོན་སློབ་འགས་སྐོར་ཙམ་ཕྱིན་པས་གནས་ཚུལ་ངེས་པར་བྱུང་བ་ལགས་སོ།

ཐར་དགོན་སྨན་ལུང་འཕྲུལ་གྱི་ལྷ་ཁང་མཇལ།།
ཕ་མེས་བརྒྱུད་པས་བསྟེན་པའི་མགོན་གཉན་དེ།།
སྔན་དར་བ་ལེང་རྒྱ་མཚོས་མཆོད་བྱས་ཏེ།།
བསྟན་པ་བསྲུང་བའི་འཕྲིན་ལས་བཀའ་བསྒོ་བྱས།།

Then we arrived at Samding Monastery, established a connection with the place that night, and stayed. The next day we visited its Potrom protector chapel of the Nigu lineage and the hermitage's temple, chapel of the protectors, and so forth. From the Dharma lord, we teacher and students requested the Dharma connection of a guruyoga. When I privately requested the ritual permission of the White Protector, he did not give it, but he favored me with the ritual permission of Lhachen Palbar, the protector of Tsi.

Then we visited the temples and chapels of Tsi Nesar. The ruler Sönam Rabten greeted us with a perfect welcoming reception and in other ways. I had a niece in Dölchung who sent two horsemen for the specific purpose of calling me, insisting that I absolutely must come. So we left everyone there. A few of us, teacher and students, went briefly and ascertained the real situation.

I visited the magical temples
of Tarpa Monastery and Menlung.

To the awesome protector
my ancestral lineage trusts,
I offered a sea of ceremonial
scarves and sacrificial cakes

དེ་ནས་པ་རྣམ་རྫོང་གི་གཞུང་དུ་ཕྱིན།།
འཁོར་རྣམས་གཏོར་ཚོགས་མེད་པའི་ཇ་གཤང་གི།
སྒྲ་དབྱངས་སྙིག་པའི་བྱ་རོག་བཞིན་དུ་འགྱོད།།
ཁོ་བོ་ཕོ་ཚོད་ཆེ་བའི་ཁྲིམ་ཐོག་ཆོད།།

ཕྱིན་ཆད་ཕྱོགས་འདིར་འོང་བའི་རྣལ་འབྱོར་རྣམས།།
འདི་འདྲའི་རིགས་ལ་རིམ་པ་ལྟར་འཛོམས་མཛོད།།
ཟེར་བའི་རྒྱང་སྒྲ་ལེན་ཞིང་བསམ་ཕྱིངས་ཀྱི།།
རི་ལ་འཛོགས་པས་ལུགས་གཉིས་འདོད་པ་ཚེམ།།

ཡང་སྨྲས་པ།

ཉང་སྟོད་ཀྱི་ཨ་མོ་འདོལ་ཆུང་ན།།
ཚ་མོ་ཞིག་ཡོད་པས་ནན་གྱིས་བོས།།

ཇན་ཆེན་དང་གཞིས་ལེན་བསྲེས་སེ་བ།།
ཁྲམ་དུས་ཀྱི་ཁ་རྒྱན་བཅས་པ་བྱུང་།།

and commanded his deeds
of guarding the doctrine.

Then inside the fortress
of Panam we went.

Like ravens arriving
at the melody of drums
and gongs when there's
no pile of sacrificial cakes,
my followers were disappointed.

I became famous
for great confidence.

"From now on, yogins
coming in this direction,
avoid this type like the plague!"

Singing that song from afar,
I climbed Mount Samding,
and our wishes in both
traditions were fulfilled.

གཏེར་སྒྲིན་འདྲ་ཡོང་སླམ་ཡོད་ཚོད་གདའ།།
ང་རྒྱལ་ཁམས་ཀྱི་ལོངས་སྤྱོད་ཆར་ལྟར་བབས།།

ཆོས་ལྡན་གྱི་འགྲོ་ས་ཚོགས་ལས་མང་།།
དཔོན་ངན་གྱི་ཁྲལ་འབབ་ཡོང་དོན་མེད།།
ཚོན་པོ་ལ་སྐྱུམ་བཀུས་མ་རེ་མཛོད།།

Tsi Nesar

I would also say:

At Amo Dölchung
in upper Nyang, a niece
of mine insistently called.

A mixture of scorn
and welcome ensued,
topped off with deception.

She apparently thought
I might come as a treasure giver.

But the riches of the country
have fallen on me like rain.

There're so many places to go
where there are Dharma practitioners.

To the tax collection of bad
chieftains, it's not worth coming.

Please don't hope to add oil to fat!

དེ་ནས་བོད་ཀྱི་ལྷ་བཙན་པོའི་གདུང་བརྒྱུད་དྲི་མ་མེད་པ་སྐྱ་བོ་བྱང་ཆུབ་སེམས་དཔའི་མཛད་པ་ལྟར་ལེན་པ། འབྲོང་རྩེ་ནས་ཁྲི་ནམ་མཁའ་བསོད་ནམས་ཀྱི་དྲུང་བཞུགས་པའི་གཞིས་ཀ་རྣམ་སྲས་མཐོང་སྨོན་དང་ཁད་ཉེ་བ་ཞིག་ཏུ་སླེབས། སུ་ཡིན་རྩད་གཅོད་མི་གནང་བྱུང་བས། དཔལ་ལྡན་ས་སྐྱ་སྐོར་ནས་ཡིན་ཟེར་བའི་བརྫུས་སེ་བ་ཞུས་ཀྱང་དགོངས་ནས་ཅིས་ཀྱང་ཤོག་གསུངས་ནས་ཕྱིན། ཞབས་ཏོག་གཞིས་ལེན་ཡང་དག་ཐུགས་དཀར་བས་ཀུན་ནས་བསླངས་པ་མཛད།

སྡེ་པའི་དྲུང་དུ་པདྨ་དབང་ཆེན་ཡང་གསང་ཁྲོས་པའི་དབང་བཞི་ཡོངས་སུ་རྫོགས་པ། བཀའ་སྡོད་རྣམས་ཀྱི་སྲོག་དབང་སོགས་ཕུལ། གཞན་ཡང་འདོད་ཆོས་ཀྱི་ཐུགས་བཞེད་མང་པོ་འདུག་པ་ཡར་ལམ་འབུལ་བའི་ཁས་ལེན་ཞུས་ནས་རྒྱལ་མཁར་རྩེར་ཕྱིན་

རྫོང་རྒྱབ་ཏུ་ཞྭོག་གྲྭ་བྱས་བསྡད་པས། གནས་ཆེན་པས་ཅིས་ཀྱང་ཡོང་དགོས་གསུངས། དཔལ་འཁོར་བདེ་ཆེན་གྱི་ཤག་ཏུ་བོས་གཞིས་ལེན་མཛད། ནང་སོས་སྣེ་སྦྱོར་མཛད་ནས་ཆོས་སྡེའི་ལྷ་ཁང་སྟེང་ཤོད། མཆོད་རྟེན་ཆེན་པོ། རྒྱལ་རྩེའི་ལི་མ་ལྷ་ཁང་། གཟིམས་ཆུང་སྟེང་ཤོད་འགའི་རྟེན་རྣམས་ཞིབ་པར་མཇལ།

རྒྱལ་རྩེ་ནས་སྡེ་པ་ཆེན་མོ་དེ་ཉིན་རེ་བཞིན་ཆོས་སྡེ་ལ་ཞབས་སྐོར་ལ་སྒྲིགས་བཅུག་ཕེབས་པ་མཐོང་བས། དེང་སང་གི་ཨ་པོ་ཏོར་འདྲའི་དོན་སྐྱི་ཡོད་པ་ཞིག་མི་འདུག་ནའང་། ཆོས་རྒྱལ་གྱི་མཛད་སྤྱོད་སྐྱོ་སུན་མེད་པར་བསྒྲིགས་སུ་བཅུག་པ་འདི་ཙམ། རང་ཐོག་ཏུ་བབས་ནའང་ནུས་པ་དཀའ་བས་ངེས་པར་ཆོས་རྒྱལ་དུ་འདུག་སྙམ་པའི་དག་སྣང་ཆེན་པོ་བྱུང་།

དེ་རྗེས་འབྲུག་པ་ངག་དབང་ཆོས་རྒྱལ་དང་དེ་གོང་ནས་གསུང་ཆོས་ཀྱི་འབྲེལ་པ་ཡོད་

Then we arrived at a spot near the Namsé Tongmön estate, where the honorable Tri Namkha Sönam from Drongtsé resided. He was in the immaculate hereditary lineage of the divine monarchs of Tibet and maintained the behavior of a layman bodhisattva. When he sent a man to investigate who we were, we disguised ourselves by saying we were from around Sakya. But after some consideration he said we certainly had to come, so we went. With sincere motivation he presented perfect service and welcome.

To the ruler I offered the complete four initiations of Pema Wangchen Yangsang Tröpa, the life-force initiation of the guardians, and so forth. Furthermore, he had many ideas about Dharma teachings that he wanted. I agreed to offer them on the way back, and we went to Gyalkhar Tsé.

When we pitched the tents behind the fortress and stayed there, the great lord of the place said I certainly had to come. He called me to the residence of Palkhor Dechen and welcomed me. The governor acted as a guide, and I carefully visited the upper and lower temples of the abbey, the great stūpa, the Gyantsé temple of bronzes, and sacred objects in several of the upper and lower apartments.

When I saw that great ruler coming routinely, every day, from Gyantsé to the abbey to perform circumambulations, I thought with deep appreciation, "Even if he does lack the attitude of the rough men these days who act like Mongols, just this ordinary conduct as a Dharma king without weariness and discomfort would be difficult to bear if I had to do it. So he is certainly a Dharma king."

After that, I had the wish to visit Drukpa Ngawang Chögyal (because I had a connection of Dharma teachings from him before) and, along with touring Ralung, to enter into Yamdrok through Kharo and gradually visit such places

པས་མཛལ་བ་དང་ར་ལུང་བསྐོར་བ་སྤྲགས་མཁའ་རོ་ནས་ཡར་འབྲོག་གི་ནང་ལ་ཞུགས། དོ་རི་སོགས་གནས་མཛལ་རིམ་པར་བྱེད་འདོད་ཡོད་ནའང་གྲྭ་པ་རྣམས་ཀྱང་མགྱོགས་སྐོར་ལ་དགའ་བ་ཙམ་འདུག་ཅིང་། ངེད་རང་གི་ཀང་ཚབ་ཀྱི་རྟ་དེའང་བབས་ཀྱི་རྣམ་པ་ཡོད་པ་ཞིག་བྱུང་བ་སོགས་ཕྱོགས་དུ་མ་ནས་མདོར་བསྟན་པས་འཕྲེད་ལ་བཅད་དེ་རོང་ཆུང་ལ་འགྲོ་བའི་གྲོས་ཐག་བཅད་དོ།

བོད་རྒྱལ་པོ་གཞོན་ནུས་གཙུག་གིས་མཆོད།།
ཤར་རྒྱལ་པོའི་མཛོད་པས་ཡིད་རབ་ཕྲོགས།།
རྟ་མདོ་ཕྲུག་གི་བང་འགྲོས་དེ་ཙ་ཟད།།
ཁོང་གྲྭ་པ་ཀུན་ཟ་ཐག་ཉེ་ལ་དགའ།།

དཔལ་ར་ལུང་གི་རི་ཁྲོད་ལྷ་བ་དང་།།
ཕ་ངག་དབང་ཆོས་རྒྱལ་མཇལ་སྐམ་ཆེ།།
ལུས་འཕོས་མེད་ཀྱི་ཀང་པས་རང་མཚང་བསྟན།།

ང་ལུགས་གཉིས་ཀྱི་སྣང་དོར་མི་ཞན་ཀྱང་།།
ལུས་ཀང་པའི་འཁྲུལ་འཁོར་འདོར་ལེན་བྲལ།།

ཁོང་དུད་འགྲོ་ལ་འགྲོ་འདུག་གི་སྐྱབས་གནས་འཚོལ།།
ང་མི་ཕྱེད་དུ་འདུག་སྐམ་སྐིད་ཁོང་གྲང་།།

as Dori. For a number of reasons, however (in brief, such as the monks only wanting a quick tour and the horse that was the substitute for my leg being in bad shape), I decided to cut straight across and go to Rongchung.

A young king of Tibet
paid homage
with the crown of his head.

The Shar king's deeds
enthralled me.

The racing of the colts
ended there.

Those monks were all
glad that food was nearby.

When I thought to see
the hermitage of glorious Ralung
and visit father Ngawang Chögyal,
my body's feeble leg revealed its own flaw.

My acceptance and rejection
in both traditions wasn't weak,

ད་ཡང་ཞིག་བསམ་པ་འདི་ལྟར་ཤར།།

གནས་ལུགས་ལ་ལྟ་བའི་མིག་ཡོད་ན།།
ཆུ་བུར་གྱི་ཁྲ་ཧྲིག་མེད་ཀྱང་ཆོག།

ཅི་བསམ་ཀུན་འགྲུབ་པའི་བློ་ཡོད་ན།།
ཤ་ཟུས་ཀྱི་ཆང་པ་མེད་ཀྱང་ཆོག།

སེམས་ཉིད་ཀྱི་ཡང་དགོན་མཐོང་ཙ་ན།།
ར་ལུང་གི་རི་ལྟས་དེ་གར་གདའ།།

དད་མོས་ཀྱི་རང་ཞལ་མཇལ་ཙ་ན།།
མཚན་ལྡན་གྱི་བླ་མ་དེ་གར་གདའ།།

གང་བྱུང་གིས་ཆོག་ན་ཅི་བྱས་བདེ།།

བྱ་བཏང་གི་བློ་སྣ་གང་ཤར་ཡིན།།

འགྱུར་མེད་ཀྱི་བདེན་གྲུབ་མེད་པས་འཚོངས།།

རོང་ཆུང་ལ་སྤྲང་པོའི་ལམ་སྣ་ཟུག།

but the trickery of my leg
was beyond rejecting and accepting.

It trusted an animal
as its source of refuge
for moving and staying.

Thinking I was but half a man,
the center of my heart grew cold.

Now again thoughts
dawned in this way.

If I have the eye
to see the way things are,
that's enough—even
without these fleshy staring eyes.

If I have a mind
to accomplish whatever
I intend, that's enough—
even without a leg
of flesh and bone.

Yamdrok

When seeing the hermitage
of the essence of mind,
the mountain vista
of Ralung is right there.

When meeting the true
face of faith and devotion,
the authentic master is right there.

If whatever happens is enough,
you'll be happy in anything you do.

That's the random dawning
of a mendicant's thoughts.

I'm content
with nothing established
as immutable truth.

The tip of the beggar's
trail touched Rongchung.

དཔལ་འཁོར་བདེ་ཆེན་དུ་བསྡད་པའི་དགོང་དེ། ངེད་ནི་གནས་ཆེན་པའི་མཁར་ལས་བྱེད་སྐྱང་གི་ནང་ཚུ་ལག་པ་དང་ཐུག་ཆོམ་གྱིས་ཁེངས་པ་དེར་ནན་མེད་བྱས་བསྐོར་བས་ཞི་སྲུན་ལ་ཆོག་པ་ཟ། ཀླུ་བོ་རྣམས་ནི་དེའི་ནུབ་ཆར་ལྷགས་འདྲིས་པ་ཞིག་གིས་ལྷོག་པུ་རྣམས་བསྐྱེལ། འདམ་བག་གི་དཀྱིལ་དུ་ཉལ་དགོས་བྱུང་འདུག ངེད་རྣམས་ཆོས་སྡེའི་སྒོར་འཛོམས་ཙ་ན་ཐམས་ཅད་ཕར་ཡུས་ཚུར་ཡུས་སུ་འདུག་པས། ངས་ཁ་མ་བླངས་པར་སྔོན་ལ་ཐལ་ལེ་ཕྱིན།

ཉང་སྟོད་གུ་ལའི་ཤུ་དེ་ན་ཕོ་རོག་མདོ་སྟེ་མགོན་པོ་བྱ་བའི་གྲུབ་ཐོབ་ཅིག་གི་སྐུ་འདྲ་སྙན་གྲགས་ཅན། མགོན་ཁང་དང་བཅས་པ་འདུག་པ་མཇལ། དེ་ནུབ་དཔོན་སློབ་ཐམས་ཅད་རྣམ་སྲས་མཐོང་སྨོན་དུ་འཛོམས། སང་མཁར་ཁའི་མདུན་མན་ལུང་དགོན་པའི་འཁྲིས་ལ་བྱས། ཐུ་ཅུ་སྟག་ཚལ་ཟེར་བའི་ལུང་ནང་དུ་ཞག་གཅིག་བསྡད།

སང་དེ་སྟ་བར་ལ་ཤིན་ཏུ་ཆེ་བ་ཞིག་བརྒྱལ་ཕྱིན་པས། རོང་ཤམ་རྫར་གྱི་དགོན་པར་ཚ་བ་འཁྱི་བ་ལ་སླེབས། ཤམ་རྫར་ཆོས་རྗེའི་དྲུང་དུ་མཇལ། མགོན་པོ་སྟག་ཞོན་འཁོར་བཅས་ཀྱི་དབང་རྗེས་གནང་། རོང་པའི་སྟག་ཞོན་གྱི་ཤུར་དབང་དུ་གྲགས་པའི་རྟེན་མཇལ་བཀའ་

During that evening we stayed at Palkhor Dechen, I acted casual in the midst of the great lord of the place's construction work, which was full of compulsory laborers and booms and bangs. But I was wearied and upset that they were threshing. That night a combination of rain and wind flattened the little tents of my companions. They had to sleep in the middle of the mud. When we gathered at the gate of the abbey, they were all boasting back and forth, so I just went straight ahead without getting involved.

In that high valley of the Gu Pass in upper Nyang, I visited the famous image of an adept known as Porok Dodé Gönpo and the chapel of the protectors. That night all of us, teacher and students, gathered at Namsé Tongmön. We spent the next day beside Menlung Monastery, in front of Kharkha. We stayed for a day and night down in the valley called Taktsal.

Early the next day we crossed a soaring pass and thereby arrived too late for the meal at Shambhar Monastery in Rong. I met the honorable Dharma lord of Shambhar. I requested the initiation and ritual permission of the protector Takshön and his retinue, asked to visit the sacred object famed as the powerful dagger of the Rongpa Takshön, and gave commands. I respectfully explained why I needed to return later to request the complete Dharma cycle of that Dharma

བསྔོ་དང་བཅས་པ་ཞུས། ཆོས་སྐྱོང་དེའི་ཆོས་སྐོར་ཚང་མ་དང་། ཞལ་བཞི་པའི་ལས་མཁན་པུ་ཏྲ་ནག་པོ་རྣམས་ཞུ་བའི་རྗེས་སུ་སླེབས་པའི་རྒྱུ་མཚན་ཕུལ། ཞལ་བཞེས་ཀྱང་ཕེབས་སོ།

ལྷ་སྔོན་ཤམ་ཧྨར་མགུལ་གྱི་དགོན་པར་སླེབས།།
འབྲུལ་ཞིག་བླ་མའི་ཞལ་བཟང་མངོན་དུ་བྱུས།།

ཕ་མེས་བརྒྱུད་ཀྱི་སྲུང་མ་ནག་པོ་དེའི།།
སྐུ་བརྙན་མཐོང་ཞིང་དབང་དང་རྗེས་གནང་ཐོབ།།

དེ་ནུབ་གནས་དེར་ཉལ་བའི་འཆར་སྣོ་ལ།།
གཉིད་འཆག་ཐོག་འཚོག་བ་སྤུ་ཟིང་ངེ་བ།།
མངོན་སུམ་རྨི་ལམ་གང་ཡང་མ་ཡིན་པའི།།
འོག་འགྱུའི་ཚུལ་གྱི་ཟ་ཟེའི་འཆར་ཚུལ་ནི།།
གསུར་དུད་མེ་དམར་འཚུབ་མའི་ལུང་སྟོང་ན།།
སྟག་ཆེན་སྨྱོན་པ་ཞོན་པའི་མོན་ནག་ཅིག།
བསྟན་དགྲ་དམ་ཉམས་འཚོལ་ཟེར་རྒྱུག་ཅིང་འབྲལ།།
སྟོང་གསུམ་ཁྲུ་སྒྲས་འགེངས་ཤིང་ཡོད་དོ་སྙམ།།

protector and to request the black Putra who is the henchman of Caturmukha. He also agreed.

We arrived
at the monastery
on the slope
of Lhanyen Shambhar.

The fine face of
the master for whom
confusion has vanished
came into view.

I saw the image
of that black guardian
of my ancestral lineage
and received initiation
and ritual permission.

Sleeping in that place
that night, I experienced
a flash of lightning
that broke my sleep,
body hairs quivering on end,

རིས་འགའ་ཞིངས་པ་ཁྲི་ཁྲིད་མང་པོ་ཡིས།།
རི་དྭགས་འདེད་ཅིང་ཤྭ་བའི་དམར་སྐྱོག་དང་།།
གཞན་ཡང་སྟག་གཟིག་དོམ་དྲེད་བྱི་འུག་སོགས།།
རྒྱུག་འབྲལ་འཕུར་ལྡིང་བན་བུན་ཟ་ཟི་ཡིས།།
ནམ་ལངས་བར་དུ་ཐུབ་པའི་འཁྲུལ་སྣང་བྱུང་།།

དེ་དག་ཞིགས་པར་བསམ་ཚེ་ཕ་རྒོད་རྗེའི།།
བསྟན་སྲུང་མཆོག་འདི་མངོན་སུམ་ཞལ་གཟིགས་ནས།།
སྒོས་དགྲ་ཁ་ཁྲིར་ཁྲུར་ནས་ཟ་བ་སོགས།།
འཇིགས་སུ་རུང་བའི་ལས་རྗེས་མངོན་དུ་བསྟན།།

དེ་ཡི་རིག་འཛིན་རྣལ་འབྱོར་བདག་ཡིན་པས།།
ད་དུང་འདི་ཡིས་དམ་ཉམས་མང་པོ་ལ།།
དྲག་པོའི་ལས་སྦྱོར་འགྲུབ་པའི་ལྟས་སུ་གོ།

and the chaotic images that swam
up from below were real,
in no way just a dream.

In an empty valley
churning with scarlet flames,
a burning stench, and smoke,
a black savage mounted
on a giant mad tiger busily
raced about, saying, "I seek
enemies of the Buddhist doctrine
and violators of the sacred
commitments."

I thought the three-
thousandfold universe
was filled with death rattles.

Sometimes, guided by dogs,
many hunters chased wild beasts,
and the flesh of deer rotted.

The Dharma Protector Takshön

Tigers, leopards,
tawny bears, snow bears,
owls, and so forth busily
raced about, flew, and soared.

Fleeting, chaotic, confusing
appearances lasted till dawn.

Carefully pondering
them, I understood that,
after the lord, the wild father,
had directly seen the face
of this sublime guardian
of the Buddhist doctrine, he directly
revealed the terrifying effects
of his deeds, such as taking,
carrying away, and eating
specific enemies, and because I,
a yogin, am his awareness holder,
those were omens that I'd yet
impose by this means
the meting out of terrible acts
on many violators of sacred commitment.

དེ་ནས་ཤ་རའི་གྲུ་ལྕགས་ཐོན་པས། དེའི་གྲུ་ཤན་གྱི་རྟ་མགོའི་ངོས་ལ་རིན་སྤུངས་ནས་སྐྱེ་པའི་བཀའ་ཤོག་ལྕགས་ཞིབ་ལ་གཟོང་རིས་བྲིས་པ་གསེར་ཆུས་བྱུགས་པ་ལ། གྲུ་ལྕགས་འདི་དགེ་རྒྱན་ལ་བཙུགས་པ་དང་། མཉན་པ་ལ་བཞི་ཟུར་ན་བྱིན་ཡོད་པས། ཟ་འདོད་ཀྱི་གཙེར་བ་བྱུང་ན་ངོ་བསྲུང་མེད་པའི་ཞུ་བས་སློབས་པ་གྱིས། ཕྱིས་འདོམས་པའི་ཁྲིམས་ལུགས་བྱེད་ཟེར་བ་གཟེར་གྱིས་བསྡམས་ནས་བརྒྱབ་འདུག་ཅིང་།

མཉན་པ་དེ་རྣམས་ཀྱང་སྔ་གོང་དང་མི་འདྲ་བའི་ངོ་གནོང་བ་བྱས། ལྟོགས་འདོད་ཆུང་ཟད་བྱེད་འདོད་པའང་གནང་སྦྱིན་ཞུ་བ་ཡིན་ཟེར་བ་ལས་མི་འདུག་པས།

གཞིས་ཀ་རིན་སྤུངས་པ་ཁྲིམས་དམ་ཟེར་བའི་སྐད་གྲགས་བདེན་པར་འདུག རྒྱལ་པོ་ཁྲིམས་ལུགས་ཡོད་པའི་ས་ཕྱོགས་འདི་འདྲ་བ་ཞིག་ཡོང་བ་ཡིན། སྐོམས་ཆུང་ལམ་བདེ་བ། ཟས་ལྡན་གློ་བདེ་བ་སོགས་བསོད་ནམས་དཔག་མེད་འོང་བ་འདུག ངོ་མཚར་སྐམ་པས་སྐྱེ་པ་ལའང་དག་སྣང་ཅི་ཡང་སྐྱེས།

དེ་ནུབ་འབྲས་ཡུལ་སྐྱིད་ཚལ་དུ་སླེབས། གྲྭ་པ་རྣམས་ཤོལ་རགས་ཆེན་པོ་དེར་ལྡོག་གྲྭ་བྱས། སྐྱེར་གྱིས་མཁྱེན་རབ་ཆོས་རྗེའི་དགོན། ངེད་ཁའུ་བྲག་རྫོང་པའི་གྲྭ་རིགས་ཀུན་གྱི་གཙུག་རྒྱན་རྗེ་བྲག་དཀར་རབ་འབྱམས་པ་བཞུགས་པའི་གཟིམས་སྤྱིལ་དུ་ཕྱིན་ནས་མཇལ། དད་པ་དང་དག་སྣང་བསམ་གྱིས་མི་ཁྱབ་པས་ཞལ་འཛོམས་འབེལ་གཏམ་འར་མ་ཙུར་མ་བྱས་སྐྱིད་ཚལ་བའི་གྲྭ་པ་སྔགས་ཆོས་ཀྱི་འདོད་ཞེན་ཆེ་བ་མང་དག་ལའང་རྗེས་གནང་རིག་གཏད་ལུང་སོགས་མང་པོ་བྱས།

དེའི་ཚེ་ཀརྨ་པ་མི་བསྐྱོད་རྡོ་རྗེ་གཞུ་ལུང་པར་ཕེབས། སྐྱེ་པ་རིན་སྤུངས་པས་གདན་

Then we came to the boat landing of Shara. On the side of the horse-head prow of its ferryboat was the ruler's decree from Rinpung, etched with a chisel on an iron plate and painted with liquid gold. Nailed with a spike, it said, "This boat landing was established to promote virtue, and a quarter of the toll is given to the boatmen separately. If greedy harassment occurs, come and report it, speaking frankly. Later, we will administer the code of law."

Unlike before, those boatmen behaved meekly. They wanted to act a little greedy but did no more than say, "We request a tip."

The reputation of the lord of the Rinpung estate for having strict laws was true. A region with a royal code of law becomes like this. Boundless merits ensue, such that humble people travel easily and prosperous people are mentally at ease. I thought it was marvelous and felt various sorts of deep appreciation for the ruler.

That night we arrived at Kyetsal in Dreyul. The monks pitched the tents in that large fenced area below. I went privately to the residence and met Lord Dragkar Rabjampa, the nephew of Khyenrab Chöjé and the crown ornament of all we Khau Drakzongpa monks. With inconceivable faith and deep appreciation, I engaged in all kinds of discussions while in his presence. To many Kyetsal monks who had great desire for the mantra teachings, I also gave many ritual permissions, bestowals of pure awareness, reading transmissions, and so forth.

At that time, Karmapa Mikyö Dorjé had arrived in the Shu Valley. The Rinpung ruler, planning to extend an invitation, had levied a tax on all his lay and monastic subjects for the services, the welcoming, and so on. Everyone was making a noisy fuss, alternating between joy and sorrow. The teachers and students

འདྲེན་ཞུ་རྩིས་དང་། མངའ་ཞབས་ཀྱི་སྐྱ་སེར་ཐམས་ཅད་ལ་ཞབས་ཏོག་དང་བསུ་བ་སོགས་ཀྱི་ཁྲལ་བརྒྱབ། ཐམས་ཅད་དགའ་བ་དང་སྐྱོ་བ་སྤེལ་མའི་ཚུར་དེང་བ་འདུག འབྲས་ཡུལ་བ་དཔོན་སློབ་ཀྱུང་དེ་གའི་གྲབས་ཡུལ་ཁུར་ཆེ་བ་སྒྲོ་སེག་གེ་བ་ཡོད་འདུག་པས།

ངེད་ཀྱི་བསམ་པ་ལ་འབྲས་ཡུལ་བའི་ཚན་འདི་དཔོན་སློབ་སྦྱིན་བདག་ལ་བསྟེན་པའི་ཁྲལ་འབབ་ཙམ་ནི་མི་བྱེད་ཁ་མེད་དུ་འདུག དེ་ཙམ་གྱི་དང་དོད་རང་བྱེད་པའི་འབྲེལ་མེད་དམ་སླམ་པ་ཤར།

ངོ་ཤེས་ཕྲད་པ་རྣམས་ཁྱེད་གཛ་པ་མཇལ་ལས་ཆེ་ཟེར།
འཕྲུལ་དེ་ཙམ་བྱེད་ཟེར་བ་ཙམ་བྱུས།

དོན་ལ་གཛ་པ་རང་སྐྱེས་བུ་དམ་པ་ཡིན་ཉེན་ཡོད་མོད། ངེད་རང་གི་ཐོས་ཚོད་ལ་དཔགས་པའི་ལྷན་སྐྱེས་ཀྱི་ཤར་ཚོད་གཛ་པའི་རྩ་བ་རང་དྭགས་པོ་རིན་པོ་ཆེའི་སློབ་མའི་གཙོ་བོ་ཁམས་པ་མི་གསུམ་དུ་གྲགས་པའི་ནང་ཚན། དུས་གསུམ་མཁྱེན་པ་ཁམས་པ་དབུ་སེ་ཟེར་བ་དེ་ཡིན་པས། ཁོང་རྣམས་ལ་བབས་ཐོབ་བྱེད་ན། རྒྱ་གར་གྱི་ནཱ་རོ་མཻ་ཏྲི་སོགས་ཀྱི་གདམས་པ་བོད་ཡུལ་གྱི་མར་པ་མི་ལ་སོགས་ནས་བརྒྱུད་པའི་སྒྲུབ་བརྒྱུད་བཀའ་བབས་ཆུ་བོའི་གཞུང་ལྟ་བུ་ཞིག་ཡོད་པས། དེ་གཙོ་བོར་སྐྱོང་དགོས་རྒྱུ་ཡིན་པ་ལ།

དགོས་པའི་མཆོད་རྟེན་ནག་པོར་བཞག མི་དགོས་ཐྲག་ལ་དབུ་དཀར་གསོལ་བའི་དཔེའི་རྣམ་པས་ས་སྐྱ་པ་དང་། དགའ་ལྡན་པ་སོགས་གང་བྱེད་ལ་མི་བསྒོ་བཞིན་དུ་འགྲན་པའི་རྣམ་པས་མཚན་ཉིད་དང་། སྔ་སྔོན་ངག་རྒྱུད་འཆད་ཉན་འདི་ནས་འཆད་རང་ཆེར་མེད་པའི་རྣམ་གྲངས་མང་ལ་དངོས་མ་གཙང་བ་སྨྱུག་པ་ཞིག་དང་། འཇིག་རྟེན་གྱི་དཔོན་

of Dreyul were also bubbling enthusiastically about the great burden of preparations for just that.

Thus, it dawned on me: "This population of Dreyul, and the teachers and students, have no choice but to provide a mere tax in service of the patron. But they have no reason for doing so with that much eagerness, do they?"

People I knew and met said, "You will most probably meet the Karmapa."

I replied by just saying, "I will immediately do just that."

In truth, the Karmapa himself may certainly be a holy person. According to what I have heard, it is my sincere understanding that Düsum Khyenpa, called Khampa Usé (one of Dakpo Rinpoché's group of chief disciples known as the Three Men of Kham), was the root source of the Karmapas. So to mention what they are responsible for, they have the instructions of Nāropa, Maitripa, and so forth of India, which were transmitted through Marpa, Milarepa, and so forth of the land of Tibet, the transmission of a lineage of practice like the main current of a river. So that's what they chiefly need to maintain.

Nevertheless, as in the proverb of leaving black the stūpa that's in need while whitewashing the rock that's not in need, he tries to contest whatever the followers of Sakya, Ganden, and so forth do, although he cannot compete. His works on dialectics, grammar, poetics, and the explanation and study of the tantras—which are not taught very much from this tradition—are numerous yet actually impure and corrupt. And he seems to engage in activities that increase the eight worldly concerns, such as those of a mundane great chieftain, lesser chieftain, or minor chieftain.

He ignores and discards his own lineal masters and their writings. It is said

ཆེན་དང་། དཔོན་ཆུང་དང་། ཡང་ཆུང་སོགས་ཆོས་བརྒྱུད་གང་འཕེལ་གྱི་བྱ་བ་ལྷུར་ལེན་པ་འདྲ་བ།

ཁོང་རང་གི་བརྒྱུད་པའི་བླ་མ་དང་དེ་དག་གི་གསུང་རབ་རྣམས་ལ་ཆས་ཆོས་རས་སུ་བོར་རེ་བ། དིང་སང་གཙོ་པ་རང་གི་བཤད་སྒྲུབ་ཀྱི་བསྟན་འཛིན་ཅུང་དྲག་པ་རྣམས་ལའང་སྨོད་ཅིང་། དེ་དག་གི་གྲྭ་རིགས་དྲག་པ་ཚུན་ཆད་ཁོང་རང་གི་ཕྱག་ཕྱིར་གང་ཁུགས་བྱེད་པ་སོགས་འདུག་ཟེར་བས། སྙིང་ནས་དད་པ་ལྷང་བ་ནི་མ་སྐྱེས་བྱུང་།

དེ་ཕྱིན་ངེད་རང་ས་སྐྱ་པའི་བཟའ་ཚང་མ་གཏོགས། གཙོ་པའི་ཁྲལ་འབབ་ཀྱི་ཁུར་ནི་ཅི་ཡང་མེད། དིང་སང་གི་མི་ཕལ་ཆེར་གྱིས་བྱེད་པ་ལྟར། སྔ་དཔོན་དཔོན་སྐྱ་ཞིག་གི་བླ་མ་བཙོལ་འདུག་ན་ཅིས་ཀྱང་ཆོས་ཞུ་སྙམ་པ་དང་། མཐའ་མི་མང་གིས་སྐོར་འདུག་ན་སངས་རྒྱས་ཡིན་སྙམ་རྒྱུག་པའི་གླུན་པོ་ནི་ངེད་རང་མིན། རང་གི་དགོན་ཆུང་ལ་མང་ཇ་འགྱེད་བཅས་ཡོང་ངམ་སྙམ་པ་དང་། གཞན་དགོན་ཆུང་ངམ་གྲྭ་རིགས་རེ་རེ་ཙམ་འཁོར་རེ་བའི་ཆེད་དུ་ཆོས་འབྲེལ་ཞུ་བའི་ལྟོགས་ལ་མེ་འབར་གྱི་བླ་མ་སློབ་དཔོན་ནི་མིན། ལེགས་ལེགས་ཀྱི་ཁྲལ་འཇལ་ནི་བྱེད་དོན་མི་འདུག

ལར་རྗེ་བཙུན་རྗོ་རིང་པ་ཆེན་པོ་དང་མཇལ་ནས་གསུང་ངག་རིན་པོ་ཆེ་འདི་ཐོབ་མན་ཆད། གཞན་བླ་མ་དང་གདམས་ངག་གང་ལའང་བྱང་ཆུབ་སྒྲུབ་པའི་ཆེད་དུ་མི་སྨོན་ཞིང་། འགྲམ་ཆུ་མི་ལྷང་བའི་ངེས་ཤེས་གཏིང་ཚུགས་ཤིག་ཡོད་པས་ལམ་གཞུང་བསྒྲངས་ཕྱིན།

དོན་ཀྱང་རྗེ་ཐམས་ཅད་མཁྱེན་པ་གཙོ་འཕྲིན་ལས་པའི་ཞབས་དྲུང་དུ་གཙོ་པའི་ཟབ་

that these days even the Karmapa's own holders of the doctrine of explication and practice (who are a bit better) are denigrated, while the best among their monks are drafted as his attendants and so on. So I didn't feel sincere faith.

From now on, except in consideration of Sakya followers, I have no burden of paying tax for the Karmapa. I'm not a scurrying fool who thinks that, if someone has been appointed the spiritual master of a ruling chieftain, a lay chieftain, I must request Dharma from him, and that if many people surround him, he's a buddha, which is how most people act these days. I'm not a master or teacher wondering whether my own little monastery will get tea offerings and alms, ravenous and burning to be asked for a Dharma connection with the hope of thereby obtaining other little monasteries or individual monks. There's no point paying a tax just to look good.

In general, after meeting the great venerable lord Doringpa and receiving this Precious Teaching, I've had a deeply rooted certainty, with no yearning or hunger for any other master and oral instruction for achieving enlightenment. So I've gone straight down the middle of the path.

Nevertheless, in the presence of the lord, the omniscient Karma Trinlepa, I had received many profound Dharma teachings of the Karmapas. So if he were definitely the rebirth of previous Karmapas, I thought faithlessness or disrespect would be inappropriate and did not let any arise.

Furthermore, in general, a Mahāyāna person knows all sentient beings have been our kind parents and cultivates deep appreciation. In particular, persons who have entered the gate of unexcelled secret mantra know all of what appears

ཆོས་མང་པོ་ཐོབ་པས། གཉྫ་པ་སྔོན་མ་རྣམས་ཀྱི་སྐུ་སྐྱེ་ཡིན་ཐག་ཆོད་ན་མི་བཏུབ་སྙམ། མ་དད་མ་གུས་པ་ཡི་མ་བྱུང་བ་བྱས།

དེ་ཡང་སྤྱིར་ཐེག་ཆེན་གྱི་གང་ཟག་གིས་སེམས་ཅན་ཐམས་ཅད་དྲིན་ཅན་གྱི་ཕ་མར་ཤེས་ནས་དག་སྣང་སྦྱོང་བ་དང་། བྱེ་བྲག་ཏུ་གསང་སྔགས་བླ་མེད་ཀྱི་སྒོར་ཞུགས་པ་རྣམས་ཀྱིས་ཅིར་སྣང་ཐམས་ཅད་ལྷ་དང་ཡེ་ཤེས་ཀྱི་རྣམ་རོལ་ཏུ་ཤེས་པར་བྱས་ནས་དེ་དག་ལ་དད་པ་དག་སྣང་ཚད་དུ་བསྐྱལ་ནས་སོ་སོའི་རང་ཞལ་རྗེན་པར་མཐོང་བའི་མོད་ལ་ལྷུག་པར་སྐྱོང་བ་འདི་གནད་དུ་ཡོད་པས་དེ་གའི་ངང་དུ་མཉམ་པར་བཞག་པ་ལགས་སོ།

ཛེ་ཡོངས་གྲགས་ཀྱི་སངས་རྒྱས་གཉྫ་པ།།
བོད་སྐྱེ་བོ་ཀུན་འདུད་པའི་གནས་གཅིག་པུ།།
ཁྱེད་བསླུ་མེད་ཀྱི་སྐྱེས་བུ་ཡོས་ཀྱང་ཡིན།།
ཁོང་དད་ཅན་ཀུན་འཁོར་བའི་མཚོ་ལས་སྒྲོལ།།

སེམས་ཡོག་རྟོག་གི་སྤྲིན་གྱིས་མ་བསྒྲིབས་ཀྱང་།།
ཁྱེད་མཛད་སྤྱོད་ཀྱི་རྣམ་ཐར་འོད་དཀར་གྱིས།།
ང་སྙིང་དབུས་ཀྱི་པདྨ་བཞད་མ་ནུས།།
དུས་ད་རེས་རྒྱ་ལམ་སྦྱོང་བ་ཞུ།།

is the play of the deity and primordial awareness, extend maximum faith and deep appreciation toward those appearances, and freely sustain that while nakedly seeing the true nature of each. This is the essential point, so I rested in balance in just that state.

Karmapa, lord known
everywhere as a buddha,
unique object of devotion
for all people of Tibet, you are,
of course, an infallible person.

You free all the faithful
from the sea of saṃsāra.

Clouds of wrong thoughts
had not obscured my mind,
but the white light of the story
of your deeds could not open
the lotus in the center of my heart.

At this time I beg to go
straight down the main road.

ཁོང་ཕལ་ཆེར་གྱིས་མཇལ་བ་སྟོང་ཙུར་ཡིན།།
ཁོང་ལ་ལ་དག་མཇལ་བ་དེ་ཆེ་འདོད་ཡིན།།
ཁོང་འགའ་ཞིག་མཇལ་བ་ལྟོགས་འདོད་ཡིན།།
ཁོང་དེ་འདྲ་ཚོ་སྙིང་ནས་དད་པ་མིན།།

ང་སྐད་སྟོང་ལ་རྒྱུག་པའི་ཁྱི་རྒན་མིན།།
ང་ལྟོ་ཕྱིར་དུ་རྒྱུག་པའི་སྤྲང་རྒན་མིན།།
ང་ཟོལ་ཟོག་གིས་སྐོར་བའི་བླུན་རྒན་མིན།།
ང་དགོན་ཚང་གིས་ཕོངས་པའི་བླ་རྒན་མིན།།

གནས་དཔལ་ལྡན་ས་སྐྱའི་དབེན་གནས་མཆོག།
དཔལ་ཁའུའི་བྲག་གི་ཕོ་བྲང་ན།།
རྗེ་རྣལ་འབྱོར་དབང་ཕྱུག་ཇོ་རིང་པའི།།
ཐུགས་གཅིག་ཏུ་འདྲེས་པའི་གཅེས་ཕྲུག་ཡིན།།

མ་བདག་མེད་མཁའ་འགྲོའི་ཐུགས་ཀྱི་བཅུད།།
རྗེ་རྣལ་འབྱོར་དབང་ཕྱུག་ཞལ་གྱི་རྒྱུན།།

Most people meet you
out of empty tumult.

Some people meet you
out of ambition.

A few people meet you
out of greed.

Such people are
not sincerely faithful.

I'm not an old dog
who scurries to an empty call.

I'm not an old beggar
who scurries for food.

I'm not an old fool
occupied with deceit.

I'm not an old master
lacking a little monastery.

དཔལ་ས་སྐྱའི་བླ་ཆེན་གདམས་པ་དེས།།
རྒྱུད་ཡོངས་སུ་ཚོམ་པས་གཞན་མི་སློན།།

དུས་ད་ལྟའི་ས་བརྙུས་ཀྱི་བརྡེ་ཚོ།།
ཆོས་འདི་འདྲའི་སྐལ་བཟང་མ་ཐོབ་པས།།
སེམས་ཆོས་བརྒྱུད་ལྟོགས་འདོད་ཀྱི་རྒྱུག་འབྲལ་གྱིས།།
ཡུལ་གར་འགྲོ་དང་འདིར་འགྲོ་མེད་སྙིང་རེ་རྗེ།།

རྗེ་དྲིན་ཅན་གྱི་བླ་མ་རྗེ་རིང་པ།།
ཁྱེད་བསམ་བཞིན་དུ་བཀའ་དྲིན་འཁོར་ཐབས་མེད།།

སྲུང་རང་མགོ་ཐོན་པ་བླ་མའི་དྲིན།།
དེ་དྲན་པའི་མོད་ལ་མཆི་མ་དགུ།།

ང་སྐྱུགས་མེད་ཀྱི་དད་པ་མཁའ་ལྟར་ཡངས།།
སྒོས་གཙ་པ་ལ་སྙིང་ནས་དད།།

At the glorious palace
of Khau cliffs, sublime isolated
site of the place of glorious
Sakya, I'm the cherished
child who blended as one
with the mind of the sovereign
lord of yogins, Doringpa.

The nutrient of the mind
of mother ḍākinī Nairātmyā,
the oral stream of the sovereign
Lord of Yogins, that instruction
of the great masters of glorious Sakya
fully satisfies my mindstream;
I yearn for no other.

At this time, monks
who pretend to be Sakya
haven't heard the good fortune
of a Dharma such as this,
so their greedy minds race busily
among the eight worldly concerns,
with no place anywhere to go—
how pitiful.

ཁྱེད་ཆོས་བརྒྱད་ཕྱོགས་འདོད་དོན་གཉེར་ཚོའི།།

གནས་ཚུལ་ནས་སྨྲས་པ་བཟོད་པར་གསོལ།།

Rinpung Fortress

Lord, kind master Doringpa,
I'm thinking of you
and a kindness I can never repay.

This beggar's independence
is the master's kindness.

Remembering that,
tears fall.

My unbiased faith
is as wide as the sky.

Specifically, I have
sincere faith in the Karmapa.

Please forgive my frank
comments about your greedy
pursuits involving the eight
worldly concerns.

Notes to the Translation

PAGE

27 ***Namaḥ sarva guru buddha bodhisattvabhyaḥ***: This initial homage is written in transliterated Sanskrit in the Tibetan text. It means "Homage to all masters, buddhas, and bodhisattvas."

27 **the great secret** (*gsang chen*): A term for the Vajrayāna teachings in general and, in particular, those of the Path with the Result, or Lamdré, in the tradition of the Explication for Disciples (Lam 'bras Slob bshad).

27 **Vajradhara** (Rdo rje 'chang): A name for the divine form of the dharmakāya, the ultimate source of the systems of tantra mostly translated into Tibet beginning in the eleventh century.

27 **lazy bum** (*bhu su ku*): Tsarchen mocks himself by using the Indian term *bhusuku*, designating a person who does nothing but eat and drink, sleep, and defecate and urinate.

27 **the Mangkar mansion of the region of upper Dar** ('Dar stod Mang mkhar gyi pho brang): Tsarchen was born at Mushong (Rmu gshong) in the lower Mangkar Valley, in the region of upper Dar not far from Sakya. See Ngawang Losang Gyatso, *Sunlight of the Doctrine of the Explication for Disciples*, 453.

29 **Khau cliffs in upper Drüm** (Grum stod Kha'u'i brag): Location of the ancient hermitage of Khau Drakzong (Kha'u brag rdzong) near Sakya, which became the residence of Tsarchen's teacher, Kunpang Doringpa.

29 **Lord Ngawang Drakpa** (Rje Ngag dbang grags pa): A Sakya master of the Khön ('Khon) family, Dakchen Ngagi Wangchuk (Bdag chen Ngag gi dbang phyug, d. 1544). He was the oldest of the three younger brothers of Salo Jamyang Kunga Sönam (Sa Lo 'Jam dbyangs kun dga' bsod nams, 1485–1533, twenty-third throne holder of Sakya). A learned and accomplished master, Ngagi Wangchuk was abbot of the monasteries of Tupten Namgyal (Thub bstan rnam rgyal) and Gawadong in Panam (Pa rnam Dga' ba gdong). See Jamgön Ameshap, *Fulfillment of All Needs and Wishes*, 493–94.

29 **Mañjughoṣa** ('Jam pa'i dbyangs): Another name for Mañjuśrī, the bodhisattva of wisdom.

29 **stayed for about eight years**: Tsarchen was about twenty-four years old (by Tibetan custom, which is followed in these notes) when he traveled to Ü for the first time as Dakchen Ngagi Wangchuk's attendant. During this period he received many Dharma transmissions from the Dakchen, such as the Lamdré teachings, the initiation of Rakta Yamāri and the guiding instructions of Utter Simplicity (Spros med), and the initiations of the Vajrāvalī. At the insistence of the Dakchen, Tsarchen also gave the complete Lamdré teachings in the tradition of the Explication for the Assembly (Lam 'bras Tshogs bshad) at Nālendra Monastery. When his teachings caused even more excitement than those of the Dakchen, some members of the Dakchen's retinue apparently became jealous. During this period Tsarchen also performed a Vajrabhairava retreat for five months, which resulted in a spectacular vision of that deity. The Fifth Dalai Lama says Tsarchen returned to the Tsang (Gtsang) region in the first month of the water dragon year of 1532. See Ngawang Losang Gyatso, *Sunlight of the Doctrine of the Explication for Disciples*, 481–82.

29 **the Teaching** (Gsung ngag): A special term referring to the Lamdré.

29 **Para** (Spa ra): At the invitation of the ruler of Para (Sde pa Spa ra ba) in the Tölung (Stod lung) region of Ü, Tsarchen traveled from western Tsang (Stod) and consecrated a new monastic hall of gilt images, a temple of the protectors, gave various teachings, and performed rituals. See Ngawang Losang Gyatso, *Sunlight of the Doctrine of the Explication for Disciples*, 506–8. At Para, Tsarchen also composed the exceptionally beautiful supplication to the lineage of Nāro Khecarī (with a poetic summation of the stages of the path) that Vajrayoginī practitioners still recite. See Tsarchen Losal Gyatso, *Celebration of Blooming White Lotuses*. Tsarchen's six-month stay in Ü seems to have begun not long after his full ordination in the summer of 1532.

29 **Sakya** (Sa skya): Khön Könchok Gyalpo ('Khon Dkon mchog rgyal po, 1034–1102), the father of Sachen Kunga Nyingpo (Sa chen Kun dga' snying po, 1092–1158), founded Sakya Monastery in 1073. The Sakya tradition of Tibetan Buddhism originated there. On Sachen, see the note on page 127 under *the great venerable lord of Sakya*.

31 **Like an imperial envoy at the outbreak of hostilities during a great conflict**: In 1642, when the Fifth Dalai Lama was forced to travel in a rush with troops in Tsang and was unable to

visit a sacred place as he wished, he quoted and identified with the sentiment of this lament in Tsarchen's journal. See Ngawang Losang Gyatso, *Divine Fabric of Transparency*, 224.

31 **pig year** (*phag gi lo*): Basically corresponding to the last nine or ten months of the Western calendar year of 1539 and the first two or three months of 1540.

33 **the Sage** (Thub pa): The historical Buddha Śākyamuni (ca. 566–ca. 486 B.C.E.).

33 **Tupten Gepel Monastery in Mangkar** (Mang mkhar Thub bstan dge 'phel dgon pa): Tsarchen had become abbot of Tupten Gepel Monastery high in the Mangkar Valley in 1534. He mostly stayed there until he left for the region of Ü in 1539. The years at Tupten Gepel were spent practicing meditation, teaching, composing works such as the biographies of Lord Doringpa and Dakchen Lodrö Gyaltsen, and visiting other areas in central and west-central Tibet to give initiations, guiding instructions, and textual transmissions. See Ngawang Losang Gyatso, *Sunlight of the Doctrine of the Explication for Disciples*, 510, 519.

33 **Namgyal Taktsé in upper Dar** ('Dar stod Rnam rgyal stag rtse): This palace, where Tsarchen often stayed in later years, was close to his birthplace of Mushong but up on a mountainside at the mouth of the Mangkar Valley. It was the fortress of the ruler of the Dar region, Darpa Rinchen Palsang ('Dar pa Rin chen dpal bzang), a patron of Tsarchen's activities who wrote a beautiful biographical supplication to him after the master's death.

37 **yoga of two stages**: The main two phases of the Vajrayāna practice of deity yoga. The *creation stage* involves visualization of the deity, and the *completion stage* is usually composed of meditation on subtle channels, winds, and drops, and of resting the mind in lucid emptiness.

41 **mealtime**: Tsarchen refers to meals and mealtime at several points in his journal. He and his companions were fully ordained Buddhist monks (*bhikṣu*) who ate only one daily meal and did not eat solid food after midday. If this meal were missed, they could not eat until the following day.

41 **Shang Gönpawa** (Zhang dgon pa ba): This is an epithet of the master Shangtön Chöbar (Zhang ston Chos 'bar, 1053–1135), from whom Sachen Kunga Nyingpo received the transmission of the Lamdré teachings. For the story of Shangtön's life, see Stearns 2001, 125, 143–47, and Stearns 2006, 206–7, 219–24.

41 **the great venerable lord of Sakya** (Rje btsun Sa skya pa chen po): The greatest master of the Sakya tradition, Sachen Kunga Nyingpo of the Khön family, was the third throne holder of Sakya. He was the first person to place the Lamdré teachings in writing. For Sachen's life, see Stearns 2001, 61–63, 133–55, and Stearns 2006, 213–27.

41 **the great hermitage of glorious Jonang** (Dpal jo mo nang gi ri khrod chen po): Jonang (Tsarchen actually uses the less frequent form of the name: Jomonang) is an ancient holy place of meditation practice. After Kunpang Tukjé Tsöndrü (Kun spangs Thugs rje brtson 'grus, 1243–1313) moved there in about 1292, the teachings of the *Kālacakra Tantra* and the Six-Branch Yoga became the specialties of the Jonang tradition. Tsarchen's teacher, Gorumpa Kunga Lekpa, whom he will visit later in his travels, had stepped down from the throne of Jonang twelve years earlier, in 1527. The abbot at this time was Gorumpa's chosen successor, Namkha Sangpo (Nam mkha' bzang po).

41 **the great Stūpa that Liberates on Sight** (Sku 'bum mthong grol chen mo): The huge stūpa that Dölpopa Sherab Gyaltsen (Dol po pa Shes rab rgyal mtshan) built at Jonang from 1330 to 1333. For the story of the events surrounding its construction, see Stearns 2010, 19–22.

41 **temple of the lineage of the Six-Branch Yoga** (Sbyor drug brgyud pa'i lha khang): A temple at Jonang dedicated to the lineal masters of the Six-Branch Yoga of the Kālacakra tradition.

43 ***E Ma!***: An exclamation of wonder.

43 **Nakgyal** (Nags rgyal): The mentsun (*sman btsun*) goddess Nakgyalma (Nags rgyal ma) is one of the twelve goddesses of Tibet who promised Guru Padmasambhava that they would protect the Buddhist doctrine. Nakgyal is also the name of the mountain where she resides and where the hermitage of Jonang is located. This goddess first invited Kunpang Tukjé Tsöndrü to move to Jonang and begin to teach there. The great adept Darchar Rinchen Sangpo ('Dar phyar Rin chen bzang po, thirteenth century) had previously spent many years meditating in several caves at Nakgyal. In the first four lines of Tsarchen's verses here, the last word of each preceding line is repeated as the first word of the next.

45 **Drakram Abbey** (Brag ram Chos sde): The Kālacakra master Bodong Rinchen Tsemo (Bo dong Rin chen rtse mo) founded Drakram in the thirteenth century. See Roerich 1976, 335, 783.

45 **the great yakṣa** (Gnod sbyin chen po): The protector chapel at Drakram was dedicated to the yakṣa known as Bektsé (Beg tse). Darchar Rinchen Sangpo meditated there in the thirteenth century, had a vision of Bektsé, and made him vow to serve the Dharma. Darchar's reliquary stūpa was at Drakram. See Ngawang Losang Gyatso, *Sunlight of the Doctrine of the Explication for Disciples*, 528; Ngawang Losang Tenpai Gyaltsen, *Illuminating the Marvels*, 213; and Ferrari 1958, 67, 156.

45 **the powerful, sublime adept for whom confusion has vanished, Ratnabhadra** (Grub pa mchog gi dbang po 'khrul zhig Ratna bha dra): Ratnabhadra is the Sanskrit translation of this master's Tibetan name, Könchok Sangpo (Dkon mchog bzang po). He took ordination from the master Könchok Gyaltsen (probably 'Jim Dkon mchog rgyal mtshan, the sixteenth abbot of Jonang) on the mountain of Nakgyal and studied extensively there. He received the profound teachings of Shambhala (i.e., the Kālacakra transmissions and the Six-Branch Yoga) from the king of Dharma named Namkha, who can be identified as the eighteenth abbot of Jonang, Namkha Chökyong (Rgyal ba Nam mkha' chos skyong, 1436–1507). He practiced these and gained realization of the definitive meaning. From Rikzin Sangyé Tenpa (Rig 'dzin Sangs rgyas bstan pa) Ratnabhadra received the Nyingma transmission of Rikzin Gökyi Demtruchen's (Rig 'dzin Rgod kyi ldem 'phru can, 1337–1407) treasure teaching known as *Spontaneous Unimpeded Intention* (*Lhun grub dgongs pa zangs thal*) and reached sublime realization on the basis of that practice. From the powerful lord Namgyal Sangpo (Mthu thobs dbang phyug Rnam rgyal bzang po) he received the transmission of the Hayagrīva practices known as Pema Wangchen Yangsang Tröpa (Padma dbang chen yang gsang khros pa), actualized the power of harsh mantras, and was able to command the Dharma protectors as his slaves. Ratnabhadra also spent time in the Kathmandu Valley of Nepal, where he received the Kagyü teachings of Mahāmudrā from the Tibetan master Tsangnyön Heruka (Gtsang smyon He ru ka, 1452–1507). See Tsarchen Losal Gyatso, *Supplication to the Venerable Lord for Whom Confusion Has Vanished*, 159–62. Tsarchen had received the special Hayagrīva transmissions from Ratnabhadra once before, at which time the master caused the maṇḍala of the nine deities to actually manifest. Taking the Dharma protectors by the hand, he introduced them to Tsarchen like one person introducing another and assigned them to him as his servants and messengers. See Ngawang Losang Gyatso, *Sunlight of the Doctrine of the Explication for Disciples*, 487–88, 528–29, and 564–65. The entire episode from Tsarchen's travel journal is also quoted in Ngawang Losang Tenpai Gyaltsen, *Illuminating the Marvels*, 226–27.

45 **blood-drinking deities** (*khrag 'thung lha*): The Sanskrit term *heruka* is translated into Tibetan as *khrag 'thung* ("blood-drinking"). This is a general name for wrathful deities. The "blood" is the blood of clinging to selfhood (*bdag 'dzin*).

45 **Pema Wangchen Yangsang Tröpa** (Padma dbang chen yang gsang khros pa): This special form of the wrathful deity Hayagrīva is the ultimate expression of Lotus Speech (Padma gsung), or Padma Heruka, one of the eight great yidams of the Mahāyoga class of the Nyingma tradition. See Tsarchen Losal Gyatso, *Quick Bestower of Attainments*, 281. Guru Padmasambhava is said to have emanated in the form of a mantra practitioner known as Shangtsé Dadrak (Zhang rtse Zla grags) and transmitted the teachings of Yangsang Tröpa to the Tibetan adept Darchar Rinchen Sangpo, who was meditating in a cave at Nakgyal. Darchar also received the transmission of the yakṣa Bektsé from Padmasambhava and other Yangsang Tröpa lineages from different teachers, thus becoming the holder of both the sequential (*bka' ma*) and the treasure (*gter ma*) transmissions. See Ngawang Losang Tenpai Gyaltsen, *Illuminating the Marvels*, 207–14. When practicing these teachings in retreat, Tsarchen directly saw the face and heard the words of glorious Hayagrīva and extracted treasures (*gter*) from a nearby rock face. See Tsarchen Losal Gyatso, *Sealed Secret Autobiography*, 202–3. For details of this astounding event, see Ngawang Losang Gyatso, *Sunlight of the Doctrine of the Explication for Disciples*, 500–502.

45 **the five emissaries and Rāhula** (Ging lnga Gza' gdong): The special Dharma protectors for Hayagrīva in the form known as Pema Wangchen Yangsang Tröpa.

45 **the great teacher Padmasambhava** (Slob dpon chen po Padma 'byung gnas): This Indian master was from the region of Uḍḍiyāna in the Swat Valley of present-day Pakistan. He first established Buddhism in Tibet in the eighth century. His teachings are crucial for the Nyingma tradition, but many have also been passed down in other lineages.

45 **the eight worldly concerns** (*'jig rten chos brgyad*): The eight worldly concerns are gain and loss, fame and infamy, praise and blame, and pleasure and pain.

47 **Mount Lalung** (Bla lung ri bo): Ratnabhadra's residence of Chumolung Monastery (Chu mo lung gi dgon pa) on Mount Lalung was within one day's journey of the hermitage of Jonang. See Ngawang Losang Gyatso, *Sunlight of the Doctrine of the Explication for Disciples*, 564–65.

47 **Samantabhadra** (Kun tu bzang po): A name for the divine form of the dharmakāya, and the ultimate source of the systems of tantra translated into Tibet beginning in the eighth century, which are mostly followed in the Nyingma tradition. The phrase "crazed by the nutrient of Samantabhadra's intention" (*kun bzang dgongs pa'i bcud kyis myos pa*) may also allude to Rikzin Gökyi Demtruchen's *Spontaneous Unimpeded Intention* (*Lhun grub dgongs pa zangs thal*), on the basis of which Ratnabhadra is said to have achieved highest realization.

47 **nine dances** (*gar dgu*): The nine moods of dance are attributes of semi-wrathful tantric deities. There are three of enlightened body: flirtatiousness, bravery, and ugliness; three of enlightened speech: laughter, ferocity, and fearsomeness; and three of enlightened mind: compassion, majesty, and calm.

47 **the venerable lord, great Vajradhara, the powerful expert and realized being named Kunga** (Rje btsun rdo rje 'chang chen po mkhas dang grub pa'i dbang po Kun dga'i mtshan can): Gorumpa Kunga Lekpa (Sgo rum pa Kun dga' legs pa, 1477–1544) was a master of two worlds. He was a major disciple of Dakchen Lodrö Gyaltsen, from whom he received the transmission of the Lamdré and other teachings of the Sakya tradition. He received the Lamdré from several other masters, such as Kunpang Doringpa, and achieved deep realization through practice. Gorumpa was also a main disciple of the master Namkha Chökyong, the eighteenth abbot of the great hermitage of Jonang, from whom he received all the transmissions of the Kālacakra tradition and the practices of the Six-Branch Yoga. Gorumpa was a dedicated practitioner of the Six-Branch Yoga and was the twenty-first abbot of Jonang for twelve years, from 1516 to 1527. Tsarchen's biographical supplication to Gorumpa emphasizes his master's practice and realization of the Six-Branch Yoga, which Tsarchen had received from him in 1532. See Tsarchen Losal Gyatso, *Realized Expert of the North*. For a brief sketch of Gorumpa's life, see Stearns 2006, 256–57. Gorumpa was also one of the main teachers of Tsarchen's major disciple, Jamyang Khyentsé Wangchuk ('Jam dbyangs mkhyen brtse'i dbang phyug), who wrote his biography. Gatön Ngawang Lekpa Rinpoché, perhaps the most important twentieth-century Sakya master of the Lamdré teachings, was the reincarnation of Gorumpa.

47 **the Puntsok Rabten palace of Bodong** (Bo dong Phun tshogs rab brtan gyi pho brang): Namkha Dorjé (Nam mkha' rdo rje, 1483–1550) of the Asha ('A zhwa) clan of Tsi Nesar (Rtsis Gnas gsar) built the royal fortress at Bodong. Namkha Dorjé was the father of Jamyang Khyentsé Wangchuk, the first member of the Asha clan to be born in Bodong. Khyentsé Wangchuk would meet Tsarchen there in 1541 and become his most important disciple. See Jamyang Khyentsé Wangchuk, *Marvelous Sheaves*, 15, 53. Mudrapa Chenpo (Mudra pa chen po) founded the monastery of Bodong E (Bo dong E) in 1049. Famous masters such as Pang Lotsāwa Lodrö Tenpa (Dpang Lo tsā ba Blo gros brtan pa, 1276–1342), Lochen Jangchup Tsemo (Lo chen Byang chub rtse mo, 1303–80), and Bodong Panchen Choklé Namgyal (Bo dong Paṇ chen Phyogs las rnam rgyal, 1376–1451) lived there. See Ferrari 1958, 67, 156.

47 **glorious Hevajra** (Dpal Kye rdo rje): Hevajra is one of the major deities of the highest class of Buddhist tantra. The meditative practice of Hevajra according to the Lamdré system of the great Indian adept Virūpa is crucial in the Sakya tradition of Tibet.

47 **Amitāyus longevity initiation in the tradition of the Queen of Adepts** (Grub rgyal lugs kyi tshe dbang): Rechungpa Dorjé Drak (Ras chung pa Rdo rje grags, 1083–1161), a major disciple of Jetsun Milarepa (Rje btsun Mi la ras pa, 1040–1123), brought this special practice of Amitāyus to Tibet. Rechungpa had received it in India from the yoginī known as the Queen of Adepts (Grub pa'i rgyal mo), whom the buddha Amitāyus had graced. In Tibet, it was first transmitted through various Kagyü lineages and then also passed into other traditions. Tsarchen and Jamyang Khyentsé Wangchuk both wrote texts for this practice.

47 **the initiation bell in a wooden case that I had previously offered**: This probably means Gorumpa used the bell during the initiation and returned it to Tsarchen as a special blessed object.

49 **four basic treatises** (*dka' bzhi*): The four basic treatises (also spelled *bka' bzhi*) are sometimes listed as Dharmakīrti's *Pramāṇavārttika* (*Tshad ma*), Maitreya's *Abhisamayālaṃkāra* (*Phar phyin*), Candrakīrti's *Madhyamakāvatara* (*Dbu ma*), and either Vasubandhu's *Abhidharmakośa* (*Mdzod*) or Guṇaprabha's *Vinayamūlasūtra* (*'Dul ba*). See Dungkar Losang Trinlé, *Clarification of Knowledge*, 128, under the entry for *dka' chen bzhi*. Some lists omit the *Pramāṇavārttika* and include the remaining four.

49 **Dakchen, great Vajradhara** (Bdag chen Rdo rje 'chang chen po): Dakchen Lodrö Gyaltsen (Bdag chen Blo gros rgyal mtshan, 1444–95) of the Khön family was the twenty-second throne holder of Sakya. This influential master of the Sakya tantric lineages separated the Lamdré teachings into the Explication for the Assembly and the Explication for Disciples. Two of Tsarchen's teachers, Kunpang Doringpa and Gorumpa Kunga Lekpa, were Dakchen Lodrö Gyaltsen's major disciples. For a brief sketch of Dakchen Lodrö Gyaltsen's life, see Stearns 2006, 254–55. For the definitive biography, see Tsarchen Losal Gyatso, *Garland of Captivating Water Lilies*.

49 **the governor and nobles from Nesar**: See the note on page 146 for more information about Nesar (Gnas gsar), which is the same as Tsi Nesar (Rtsis Gnas gsar). Gorumpa was the main teacher of the Asha noble family of Nesar and received their patronage. The ruler at Bodong in 1539 was the Tsi Nesar governor Namkha Dorjé (Rtsis Gnas gsar Nang so Nam mkha' rdo rje), who was Jamyang Khyentsé Wangchuk's father. He had been the interior minister (*nang blon*) for the Sengé Tsé ruler (Sde srid Seng ge rtse pa), then settled in Bodong E, and in 1516 invited Gorumpa to become abbot of Jonang. He was also a major patron of both Doringpa and Tsarchen. See Jamyang Khyentsé Wangchuk, *Rippling Ocean of Wish-Fulfilling Marvels*, 297; Jamyang Khyentsé Wangchuk, *Marvelous Sheaves*, 11–20, 136–37; and Tsarchen Losal

Gyatso, *Marvels That Cause Body Hairs to Tremble with Faith*, 233–34. Events surrounding Namkha Dorjé's death are described in Ngawang Losang Gyatso, *Sunlight of the Doctrine of the Explication for Disciples*, 591–92.

49 **royal palace of Namgyal Rabten** (Rnam rgyal rab brtan rgyal po'i pho brang): Another name for the Puntsok Rabten royal fortress at Bodong.

49 **profound definitive meaning** (*nges don zab mo*): Tsarchen's use of this phrase when praising Gorumpa alludes to the teachings on definitive meaning and the practices of the Kālacakra tradition emphasized at Jonang.

51 **whose toenails rest on the braided topknots**: It is a gesture of deep devotion to lift up the feet of one's teacher and place them on top of one's head. It is also customary in Vajrayāna practice to imagine one's teacher (often in the form of a deity) present on the crown of one's head.

51 **Dakchen Rinpoché** (Bdag chen Rin po che): The master Ngakchang Kunga Rinchen (Sngags 'chang Kun dga' rin chen, 1517–84) of the Khön family of Sakya was the nephew and main disciple of Sakya Lotsāwa (Sa Lo 'Jam pa'i rdo rje, 1485–1533), the twenty-third throne holder of Sakya. Kunga Rinchen succeeded his uncle and was the twenty-fourth throne holder of Sakya for fifty years, from 1534 until 1584. This was a period of severe troubles. He was forced into exile when the warlord Lhasa Dzongpa (Lha sa Rdzong pa, d. 1544) invaded Sakya and seized the Lhakhang Chenmo, or Great Temple. Just before these events Kunga Rinchen was staying in retreat at Geding in Shab (Shab Dge sdings), where Tsarchen met him. After some years in Ü, where he was asked to occupy the throne of Nālendra Monastery, Kunga Rinchen was finally able to return to Sakya with the help of armies that the rulers of Jang (Byang) and Gyantsé (Rgyal rtse) had raised. They defeated Lhasa Dzongpa and destroyed his fortress. Kunga Rinchen is remembered for upholding the crucial Dharma lineages of the Sakya tradition and for carrying out new construction and extensive renovations of ancient temples and buildings at both Sakya in Tsang and at Samyé (Bsam yas) Monastery in Ü. See Jamgön Ameshap, *Ocean of Marvels*, especially 95–101.

53 **Geding** (Dge sdings): Geding is about one day's travel from Bodong and quite near Tropu (see note below). See Ferrari 1958, 67, 157. Several other Sakya throne holders of the Khön family had previously lived or spent time at Geding, such as Gyagar Sherab Gyaltsen (Rgya gar Shes rab rgyal mtshan, 1436–94) and his younger brother Dakchen Lodrö Gyaltsen. Their

Rinchengang residence (Rin chen sgang bla brang) of the Khön family later became known as the Geding residence. See Tsarchen Losal Gyatso, *Garland of Captivating Water Lilies*, 54.

53 **the extensive and condensed rites of offering to the masters, which the great omniscient Dakchen had composed, and the guruyoga connected to them**: The great omniscient Dakchen (Bdag chen thams cad mkhyen pa chen po) is Dakchen Lodrö Gyaltsen. The guruyoga that he composed in connection with the Hevajra practice of the Lamdré, entitled *Lam zab mo bla ma'i rnal 'byor nyams su blang ba'i tshul bdag chen rdo rje 'chang gis mdzad pa*, is found in *Sa-skya Lam-'bras Literature Series*, vol. 20 *wa*: 1–18 (Dehra Dun: Sakya Centre, 1983). I have not been able to locate Dakchen Lodrö Gyaltsen's rites of offering to the masters (*bla ma mchod chog*).

53 **both traditions**: That is, both religious and secular customs.

53 **Tropu** (Khro phu): Gyaltsa Rinchen Gön (Rgyal tsha Rin chen mgon), a disciple of the Kagyü master Pakmodrupa Dorjé Gyalpo (Phag mo gru pa Rdo rje rgyal po, 1110–70), founded Tropu Monastery in 1171. The tradition that developed there became known as the Tropu Kagyü (Khro phu bka' brgyud).

53 **Face-Viewing Temple** (Zhal ras lha khang): The upper temple where the face of the huge Maitreya image could be viewed.

53 **fake fangs** (*krung krum*): According to Khenchen Appey Rinpoché, Tsarchen wondered whether the woman had used something like a dikon/radish (*la phug*) or turnip (*nyug ma*) to make fake fangs to frighten him. The process of determining the meaning of the obscure term *krung krum* illustrates the extreme fragility of transmission. In November 2010, when even Khenpo Gyatso (perhaps the best Sakya scholar of his generation) did not understand this term, he asked his teacher Khenchen Appey Rinpoché about the meaning and then wrote to me. Khenchen Appey Rinpoché passed away the next month. If the question had been delayed for only a few weeks, the meaning would probably have remained forever lost.

55 **Bloody Mount Sinpo** (Khrag 'dzag Srin po'i ri): Not long after the final events recorded in this travel journal, and certainly before the end of 1540, Tsarchen would visit Bloody Mount Sinpo, or Bloody Demon Mountain. Mount Sinpo is a famous holy place in Ü believed to be a palace of the deity Cakrasamvara, whose consort is Vajravārāhī, or Vajrayoginī. At Mount Sinpo, Tsarchen again saw the same frightening woman he had encountered at Tropu.

When he recognized her according to the previous prophecy and prayed to her with deep devotion, she transformed into Vajrayoginī and spoke to him. In this way, the Vajra Queen directly graced him. See Ngawang Losang Gyatso, *Sunlight of the Doctrine of the Explication for Disciples*, 558.

55 **the land of Penkar** ('Phan dkar kyi ljongs): When Tsarchen was later riding by horseback on a road in Penyul ('Phan yul), to the north of Lhasa, a mass of roaring fire appeared in the sky. As he wondered what it was, it fell in front of him on his saddle and instantly transformed into Vajrayoginī. When she embraced him, he experienced nothing but taintless ecstasy for seven days and nights. See Ngawang Losang Gyatso, *Sunlight of the Doctrine of the Explication for Disciples*, 535.

59 **the great Maitreya** (Byams chen): The Tibetan Sanskrit scholar and translator Tropu Lotsāwa Jampai Pal (Khro phu Lo tsā ba Byams pa'i dpal, 1172–1236) completed construction of this gilt copper image (about 120 feet tall) of the future buddha Maitreya at Tropu in 1212. The image is described in detail in Chökyi Gyatso, *Necklace of Moon Crystals*, 478–80.

59 **the great stūpa** (Sku 'bum chen mo): Tropu Lotsāwa Jampai Pal began the construction of this stūpa at Tropu when he was fifty-eight years old (1230) and completed the shrines on the third floor in 1234. It was built as a reliquary shrine for some of the remains and special relics of his master, the great paṇḍita of Kashmir, Śākyaśrībhadra (1140s–1225?). See Jampai Pal, *Wish-Fulfilling Vine*, 86a–87a. The stūpa of Tropu was built of stone, with three stories of five temples on each of the four sides, totaling sixty. See Chökyi Gyatso, *Necklace of Moon Crystals*, 481.

59 **the two-faced Vārāhī** (Phag mo zhal gnyis ma): The Fifth Dalai Lama describes the light above the Vajravārāhī image as a rainbow that later dissolved into Tsarchen's heart, causing him to experience only taintless ecstasy for many days and nights. See Ngawang Losang Gyatso, *Sunlight of the Doctrine of the Explication for Disciples*, 535.

59 **Queen of Khecara** (Mkha' spyod dbang mo): Khecarī, whose paradise is Khecara.

59 **Khecarī** (Mkha' spyod ma): Another name for Vajrayoginī, or Vajravārāhī. Of the Thirteen Golden Dharmas (Gser chos bcu gsum) in the Sakya tradition, three are the cycles of Khecarī from Nāropa (1016–1100), from Maitripa (1012–97), and from Indrabhūti. Tsarchen and two of his major disciples, Jamyang Khyentsé Wangchuk and Mangtö Ludrup Gyatso, wrote definitive works on the practice of Nāro Khecarī.

59 **I have a lot to say about this**: Here Tsarchen alludes to an episode from earlier in his life, which is described at the beginning of the introduction to this book. A woman had approached him at the Geluk (Dge lugs) monastery of Tashi Lhunpo (Bkra shis lhun po) and said Lord Doringpa had summoned him. She gave him a small manuscript, saying it was a gift from Doringpa. Then she vanished. Tsarchen soon set off for Khau Drakzong. When he arrived and told Doringpa what had happened, his teacher just laughed and said, "Oh, my! Khecarī went to fetch you. This book is her Dharma cycle. Take it to the bookstacks for now." Tsarchen took the book to the stacks. Among all the books there was a gaping hole where the text had been removed. When he put it back, it fit exactly into the space, and he was overcome with inexpressible faith and wonder. See Ngawang Losang Gyatso, *Sunlight of the Doctrine of the Explication for Disciples*, 466–67.

59 ***Phaṭ!***: A Sanskrit syllable forcefully enunciated for the purpose of shattering ordinary consciousness and allowing the mind to rest in the space of lucid nonconceptual awareness.

61 **Lord Sakya Lotsā** (Rje Sa skya Lo tsā): Jamyang Kunga Sönam Drakpa Gyaltsen ('Jam dbyangs kun dga' bsod nams grags pa rgyal mtshan, 1485–1533), also known as Salo Jampai Dorjé (Sa Lo 'Jam pa'i rdo rje), of the Khön family, was the twenty-third throne holder of Sakya. He also held one of the thrones at Nālendra Monastery in Ü. He was a main lineage holder of the Sakya tantric transmissions and perhaps the most important disciple of Lowo Khenchen Sönam Lhundrup (Glo bo Mkhan chen Bsod nams lhun grub, 1456–1532).

63 **Wrathful King** (Khro rgyal): An epithet of major wrathful deities, probably here signifying Hayagrīva as Pema Wangchen Yangsang Tröpa.

65 ***A La La!***: An expression of wonder.

67 **Dampa Marpo** (Dam pa dmar po): The Tibetan master Dampa Marpo met the Indian adept Padampa Sangyé (Pha Dam pa Sangs rgyas, d. 1105) in Tibet and then traveled to India and studied under Vajrāsanapāda (Rdo rje gdan pa). Dampa Marpo was a lineage holder of some special Avalokiteśvara practices. His story is found in Roerich 1976, 1025–29.

67 **Avalokiteśvara** (Spyan ras gzigs): This bodhisattva is the epitome of selfless compassion.

67 **Gangchen Chöpel Monastery** (Gangs can chos 'phel gyi dgon pa): Panchen Sangpo Tashi (Paṇ chen Bzang po bkra shis, 1410–78) founded this Geluk monastery. He was also

the second abbot of Tashi Lhunpo Monastery. A blessed image of the protector goddess Maksorma was kept at Gangchen Chöpel. See Ferrari 1958, 58, 157.

67 **goddess Maksorma** (Lha mo Dmag zor ma): A form of the protector goddess Śrīdevī (Dpal ldan lha mo).

67 **the ruler Silnönpa** (Sde pa Zil gnon pa): Long before Tsarchen's journey, the Rinpung ruler Dönyö Dorjé (Don yod rdo rje, 1463–1512) had heard of the incredible beauty of the wife of the lord of Yamdrok Nakartsé (Yar 'brog Sna dkar rtse). In a mouse year (1492?) Dönyö Dorjé went to Yamdrok with a fearsome military regiment. The Yamdrok chieftain did not show himself but sent out rich offerings (and his wife) to entertain the powerful Rinpung ruler. Dönyö Dorjé stayed for just a few days. In the next year, an ox year, a son named Silnön Dorjé (Zil gnon rdo rje) was born at Yamdrok. See Yarlungpa Abum, *Rough Genealogy of the Rinpung Dynasty*, 133. Silnön Dorjé was clearly Dönyö Dorjé's son, which explains why he was indicated in the ruler's will and called from Nakartsé to Rinpung and acknowledged as a member of the family after Dönyö Dorjé's death in 1512. See Sönam Drakpa, *Magical Key to Royal Genealogies*, 98, 100, 101, and Shakabpa, *Political History of Tibet*, vol. 1: 355. For some time, Silnönpa was a powerful ruler. But Dönyö Dorjé's cousin, Ngawang Namgyal, eventually rose to the head of the Rinpung dynasty. Silnön Dorjé requested the vows of a novice monk from the Kagyü master Treho Chökyi Gyatso (Tre ho Chos kyi rgya mtsho, d. 1547). Still known as the ruler Silnönpa (Sde pa Zil gnon pa), he later received complete ordination from the Eighth Karmapa, Mikyö Dorjé. This apparently took place in the pig year of 1539, during the Karmapa's journey to Rinpung that is the focus of the last episode in Tsarchen's journal. See Situ Panchen Chökyi Jungné and Belo Tsewang Kunkhyap, *String of Crystal Gems*, vol. 1: 641, and vol. 2: 40–41. As late as 1556, Silnönpa was the ruler at Yamdrok Taklung (Yar 'brog Stag lung), where he invited Jetsun Kunga Drölchok to his fortress to request the initiation of Ṭakkirāja ('Dod pa'i rgyal po), one of the Thirteen Golden Dharmas of Sakya. See Kunga Drölchok, *Amazing Ornament to My Autobiography*, 296.

67 **For a person with belief and devotion, it's said, the tooth of a dog became a heap of relics**: Tsarchen refers here to a traditional story that any Tibetan would probably recognize. There was once a Tibetan trader who traveled between India and Tibet. Before he left on one of his trips, his old mother asked him to bring her a relic of the Buddha Śākyamuni. But he became involved in trading and forgot her request until he returned home and she asked him, "Did you remember the relic?" The next year she again begged him to bring her

a holy relic. But again he forgot until he had returned home and the first thing she said was, "Did you bring me a relic of the Buddha?" She was very upset that he had forgotten and told him that if he forgot the next time, she would have to accept that she was just a wretched person who did not deserve to have a holy object to worship. On his third trip to India, the son again forgot about his mother's request until he was almost home. But then he saw the corpse of an old dog decomposed by the side of the road. He bent down and pulled a tooth from the dog's skull, washed it, anointed it with saffron, wrapped it in silk, and placed it in a fine container. When he reached home he gave the "tooth of the Buddha" to his overjoyed mother. She honored the tooth with offerings, circumambulations, and so forth for many years. During this time some wonderful things occurred, such as pearl-like objects being found heaped in the container with the tooth, which the mother distributed to friends as blessings. Finally, the old woman died, and several miracles occurred, such as rainbows surrounding the house. The people all said these things happened because of the great holy object, the tooth of the Buddha, which was enshrined in the house. But then the son stepped forward and said, "Nonsense! This object is not from the Buddha at all but just a tooth taken from the skull of an old dog!" The wise men of the region said, "These miracles that have occurred have nothing to do with the object but illustrate the great and profound faith of the mother."

71 **Chumik Ringmo in Tsang** (Gtsang Chu mig ring mo): With the patronage of the Mongol prince Jingim (Jim Gyim), the son of the Yüan dynasty emperor Khubilai Khan (1215–94), the Sakya master Pakpa Lodrö Gyaltsen ('Phags pa Blo gros rgyal mtshan, 1235–80) held a huge Dharma council at Chumik Ringmo in 1277. From the time of Ta En Kunga Rinchen (Ta dben Kun dga' rin chen, 1339–99), who gave extensive teachings at Chumik, up until Dakchen Chumikpa Lodrö Wangchuk (Bdag chen Chu mig pa Blo gros dbang phyug, 1402–81), many members of the Zhitok residence (Gzhi thog bla brang) of the Khön family of Sakya taught and lived at Chumik. The Zhitok residence later became known as the Chumik residence. See Jamgön Ameshap, *Fulfillment of All Needs and Wishes*, 259, 310–11.

71 **Sangkar Lotsāwa** (Zangs dkar Lo tsā ba): The Tibetan translator Sangkar Lotsāwa Pakpa Sherab (Zangs dkar Lo tsā ba 'Phags pa shes rab) lived in the mid-eleventh century. He studied with Indian masters such as Jñānaśrī of Kashmir and brought the Dharma cycle of Vaiśravaṇa to Tibet. He built a house for the homeless beggars of Lhasa, carried out restoration work in about fifteen important temples, and translated many works from Sanskrit. Sangkar Lotsāwa passed away at Chumik Ringmo. See Dungkar Losang Trinlé, *Clarification of Knowledge*, 1803, and Roerich 1976, 354–55.

71 **the Tārā of Nyan** (Gnyan sgrol): When Tsarchen visited this Tārā image, he had a dream of a young woman wearing a blue dress, who told him, "This deity was the special meditation object of the Indian paṇḍita Buddhaguhya (Sangs rgyas gsang ba) and protected Nyan Lotsāwa from fear of snakes." Tsarchen was filled with devotion and believed the image was actually Tārā herself. See Ngawang Losang Gyatso, *Sunlight of the Doctrine of the Explication for Disciples*, 541. Nyan Lotsāwa Darma Drak (Gnyan Lo tsā ba Dar ma grags) was an important Tibetan translator of the eleventh century. He studied in India for twelve years and brought the teachings of the Dharma protector Caturmukha (Zhal bzhi pa) to Tibet. In some histories Nyan Lotsāwa is said to have been responsible for the death of Drokmi Lotsāwa's ('Brog mi Lo tsā ba Shākya ye shes, 993–1077?) son, Indra, in a magical duel. See Stearns 2001, 213, and Stearns 2006, 181, 646.

71 **Pakpa Rinpoché** ('Phags pa Rin po che): Pakpa Lodrö Gyaltsen ('Phags pa Blo gros rgyal mtshan, 1235–80) of the Khön family was the seventh throne holder of the Sakya tradition. He became the spiritual master of the Mongolian conqueror Khubilai Khan, the first emperor of the Yüan dynasty (1279–1368) in China.

71 **Dakchen Rinpoché Draklopa** (Bdag chen Rin po che Grags blo pa): Drakpa Lodrö (Grags pa blo gros, 1367–1437 or 1446) of the Khön family of Sakya was born at Chumik and lived there much of the time. He studied the teachings of the Sakya tradition under masters such as Lama Dampa Sönam Gyaltsen (Bla ma dam pa Bsod nams rgyal mtshan, 1312–75) and Lama Nyamepa (Bla ma Mnyam med pa). Drakpa Lodrö was particularly expert in the practices of the Dharma protectors, which he transmitted to Taktsang Lotsāwa (Stag tshang Lo tsā ba, b. 1405). See Jamgön Ameshap, *Fulfillment of All Needs and Wishes*, 313.

71 **Ngor Ewam Chöden** (Ngor E waṃ chos ldan): Ngorchen Kunga Sangpo (Ngor chen Kun dga' bzang po, 1382–1456) founded Ngor Monastery in 1429. It became the main seat of the Ngor subsect of the Sakya tradition and an important center for study and practice of the Sakya tantric teachings, especially the Lamdré. The abbot of Ngor Monastery at the time of Tsarchen's visit was Ngorchen Könchok Lhundrup (Ngor chen Dkon mchog lhun grub, 1497–1557), the tenth abbot from 1534 to 1557.

71 **Profound Path Temple** (Lam zab lha khang): This is probably another name for the Profound Path Cave (Lam zab phug) at Ngor, originally a small sleeping cave of Ngorchen Kunga Sangpo. It contained images of the masters of the Lamdré teachings. See Ferrari 1958, 62, 147.

71 **three types of sacred objects** (*rten gsum*): The traditional representations of enlightened body, speech, and mind, the most common examples of which are images, texts, and stūpas.

71 **Temple of the Path with the Result** (Lam 'bras lha khang): This temple at Ngor contained images and relics of the masters of the Lamdré, or the Path with the Result, and of former abbots of Ngor, beginning with an image of Ngorchen Kunga Sangpo constructed just after his death. See Ferrari 1958, 62, 147.

71 **the nephew Rinchen Sengé** (Dbon po Rin chen seng ge): Rinchen Sengé was the nephew of Lhachok Sengé (Lha mchog seng ge, 1468–1535), the ninth abbot of Ngor Monastery (tenure 1516–34). Lhachok Sengé is listed among Tsarchen's many teachers, so Tsarchen and Rinchen Sengé had probably met before. The "great" nephew Rinchen Sengé (Dbon chen Rin chen seng ge) is mentioned several times in Lhachok Sengé's biography, the last time being just before the master's death in 1535. See Namkha Palsang, *Downpour of Faith*, 158, 164, and 168. The "prominent nephews" of Ngor masters were often influential figures.

71 **Pañjaranātha** (Gur mgon): The specific form of the Dharma protector Mahākāla as the special guardian of the Lamdré teachings.

73 **Shalu** (Zha lu): Chetsun Sherab Jungné (Lce btsun Shes rab 'byung gnas) built the Serkhang (Gser khang), or Golden Temple, of Shalu Monastery in 1003. See Dungkar Losang Trinlé, *Clarification of Knowledge*, 1757. The monastery was closely associated with the Sakya tradition, and a Shalu subsect developed following the time of Butön Rinchen Drup (Bu ston Rin chen grub, 1290–1364).

73 **Chaktö** (Lcags stod): Tsarchen does not name the governor at Chaktö when he visited the estate. Seventeen years later, in 1556, Jamyang Khyentsé Wangchuk visited Chaktö and offered initiations to the governor at that time, part of whose name was Namkha (Lcags stod Nang so Nam mkha'i drung). Khyentsé specifies that the governor had been born into the family of the rulers Enshrī Gyalwa Sangpo (Dben shrī Rgyal ba bzang po) and Enshrī Gyalwa Kuntu Sangpo (Dben shrī Rgyal ba kun tu bzang po). This Chaktö governor was one of the main persons who insisted that Khyentsé write his autobiography. See Jamyang Khyentsé Wangchuk, *Marvelous Sheaves*, 160, 248.

73 **the three men we Sakya followers are so boastful about**: Grand Governor Enshrī Shākya Sangpo (Dpon chen Dben shrī Shākya bzang po, in office ca. 1264–70) was first entrusted

with temporal power in Sakya when Sakya Paṇḍita Kunga Gyaltsen (Sa skya Paṇḍi ta Kun dga' rgyal mtshan, 1182–1251) left for China in 1244. Later, during the time of Sakya Paṇḍita's nephew, Pakpa Lodrö Gyaltsen, Shākya Sangpo received seals and authority from the Yüan emperor Khubilai Khan that made him the most powerful political figure in Tibet. Rinchen Tsöndrü of Tsongkha in Amdo in eastern Tibet (Shar smad Btsong kha'i dge bshes Rin chen brtson 'grus) became a learned and politically influential disciple of Pakpa. Horché Töntsul of Göngyo in Kham (Mdo stod Gon gyo'i Hor che Ston tshul) was also a learned disciple of Pakpa and spread the Sakya tradition and its political influence in eastern Tibet. See Ngawang Losang Gyatso, *Sunlight of the Doctrine of the Explication for Disciples*, 438–50, for an exhaustive account of these three figures and Tsarchen's ancestry, which is traced from Rinchen Tsöndrü. Also see various references in Petech 1990, especially 16, 19, 43–44, and 144.

73 **the lineage of the spiritual friend Rinchen Tsöndrü of Tsongkha in the east is that of my extremely close paternal relatives, in whose line Grand Governor Enshrī Gyalwa Sangpo, Hushrī Göpo Rinchen, and so on successively appeared**: As mentioned in the previous note, the spiritual friend Rinchen Tsöndrü was a learned and politically influential disciple of Pakpa. He was a monk but later took a consort and had three sons. Grand Governor Enshrī Gyalwa Sangpo (Dpon chen Dben shrī Rgyal ba bzang po) was one of Rinchen Tsöndrü's grandsons. Gyalwa Sangpo held the position of grand governor three times (1328/29–1333, 1344–47, and ca. 1350–56 or 1358) and played a crucial role in the long struggle for power between the Sakya and the Pakmodru dynasties, which resulted in the victory of Tai Situ Jangchup Gyaltsen (Ta'i Si tu Byang chub rgyal mtshan, 1302–64) and the establishment of the Pakmodru. Hushrī Göpo Rinchen (Hu shrī Rgod po rin chen), another grandson of Rinchen Tsöndrü, received the Hushrī (Chin: *fu-shih*) title and seals from the Yüan dynasty emperor Toghon Temür (r. 1333–68) and was a powerful lord. See Ngawang Losang Gyatso, *Sunlight of the Doctrine of the Explication for Disciples*, 438–50. Concerning Gyalwa Sangpo, see also Petech 1990, especially 101–10 and 116–21, and Tucci 1949, 2:687.

75 **Latö** (La stod): A general term for the western part of the Tsang region.

77 **Gyengong Temple** (Rgyan gong): The ancient temple of Gyengong is only a few hundred yards from Shalu Monastery. Lotön Dorjé Wangchuk (Lo ston Rdo rje dbang phyug) founded Gyengong in 973 with the assistance of Chetsun Sherab Jungné. The temple contains a blessed image of the Shalu Monastery protector goddess Dorjé Rabtenma (Rdo rje rab brtan ma). See Ferrari 1958, 60, 143. The woman Tsarchen sees is actually an emanation

of this goddess. According to the Fifth Dalai Lama, the event was an omen that Tsarchen would one day ascend the throne of Butön Rinchen Drup at Shalu. See Ngawang Losang Gyatso, *Sunlight of the Doctrine of the Explication for Disciples*, 542.

77 **the Mahākaruṇika of the Serkhang at the site of Shalu** (Zha lu gnas kyi gser khang gi thugs rje chen po): With the patronage of Kushang Drakpa Gyaltsen (Sku zhang Grags pa rgyal mtshan), Chetsun Sherab Jungné built the Serkhang, or Golden Temple, of Shalu Monastery in 1003. The Mahākaruṇika of the Serkhang is the main image at Shalu. Chetsun Sherab Jungné, who had gone to India and become a disciple of the famous Abhayākaragupta, brought this black stone image of Avalokiteśvara Khasarpaṇa from Bodhgayā to Tibet. See Tucci 1989, 71. Tsarchen later became the thirteenth abbot of Shalu Monastery from 1555 until 1559.

77 **Kagyü tradition** (Bka' brgyud pa): There are many different Kagyü traditions in Tibet. The most famous lineages are based on the teachings of great Indian adepts such as Saraha, Nāropa, and Maitripa. Marpa Lotsāwa Chökyi Lodrö (Mar pa Lo tsā ba Chos kyi blo gros, 1012–97) brought most of these instructions to Tibet.

77 **bearskin visor** (*dom ra*): A bearskin band tied around the forehead with the fur hanging over the eyes to prevent snow blindness.

77 **concealment wood** (*sgrib shing*): Wood from a crow's nest believed to make its possessor's body invisible when mantras are spoken over it.

77 **Ripuk** (Ri phug): In 1314 Butön Rinchen Drup constructed a large temple at this monastery in the mountains to the northwest of Shalu Monastery. See Ferrari 1958, 60, 143, and Dungkar Losang Trinlé, *Clarification of Knowledge*, 1757.

77 **the omniscient Butön** (Bu ston thams cad mkhyen pa): Butön Rinchen Drup (Bu ston Rin chen grub, 1290–1364) mostly lived and taught at Shalu Monastery. He was a great master of Buddhist doctrine in general and of the Vajrayāna in particular, especially the Kālacakra tradition. Tsarchen is believed to have been Butön in a previous lifetime. For a translation and study of Butön's biography, see Seyfort Ruegg 1966.

77 **the Nālendra Chogyé abbot** (Nā lendra'i bco brgyad pa): The holder of the Chogyé title at Nālendra Monastery at this time was either Jamyang Dönyö Gyaltsen ('Jam dbyangs don yod

rgyal mtshan, the tenth abbot of Nālendra) or Sönam Lhundrup (Bsod nams lhun grub, the eleventh abbot). I am grateful to David Jackson for this information. Tsarchen had visited and taught at Nālendra during his first trip to the Ü region during the years 1524–31. He had probably given teachings to the physician of the Nālendra Chogyé abbot at that time, since in the following verses he refers to him as a disciple of previous acquaintance.

79 **the reliquary of Sharchen** (Shar chen gyi rten): Probably the reliquary stūpa of Sharchen Yeshé Gyaltsen (Shar chen Ye shes rgyal mtshan, 1359–1406), a teacher of the Sakya master Ngorchen Kunga Sangpo.

79 **an elderly personal disciple of Khyenrab Rinpoché**: Khyenrab Chöjé Rinchen Chokdrup (Mkhyen rab Chos rje Rin chen mchog grub, 1436–97) was the first Chogyé Trichen (Bco brgyad khri chen) at Nālendra Monastery. See the note on page 153 for more about him. The Fifth Dalai Lama identifies his elderly disciple as Tashi Paljor of Chakgok Valley (Lcags sgog lung pa Bkra shis dpal 'byor). See Ngawang Losang Gyatso, *Sunlight of the Doctrine of the Explication for Disciples*, 491, 541. In the following verses of his travel journal, Tsarchen refers to this teacher as a "mendicant master" (*ku su lu'i bla ma*).

79 **Vajrapāṇi in the tradition of Sugati** (Phyag rdor 'Gro bzang): This form of Vajrapāṇi, also known as Vajrapāṇi Nīlāmbaradhara (Phyag rdor Gos sngon can), or Vajrapāṇi with the Blue Robe, comes from the Indian master Sugatigarbha (Slob dpon 'Gro bzang snying po). Sangkar Lotsāwa Pakpa Sherab brought it to Tibet in the eleventh century. See Ngorchen Kunga Sangpo, *Oceanic Record of Teachings Received*, 84.3.

79 **the ritual permissions of the calm and the wrathful Vaiśravaṇa**: Vaiśravaṇa (Rnam sras) is the protector of the northern direction. As with Vajrapāṇi in the tradition of Sugati, the ritual permissions of the calm and the wrathful forms of Vaiśravaṇa were transmitted from the Indian master Sugatigarbha. Sangkar Lotsāwa Pakpa Sherab brought them to Tibet in the eleventh century. See Ngorchen Kunga Sangpo, *Oceanic Record of Teachings Received*, 85.4–86.1.

79 **Dorjé Rabtenma** (Rdo rje rab brtan ma): A form of Śrīdevī who is the protector goddess of Shalu Monastery. Tsarchen later composed texts for her initiation and practice.

79 **tea for the road, which is crucial**: According to Dezhung Rinpoché, Tsarchen had a special love of good tea. Notice how many times he mentions tea in his brief travel journal. Tsarchen

wrote two beautiful, poetic tea offerings. Dezhung Rinpoché used to repeat the first one from memory, and Chogyé Trichen Rinpoché especially liked the second one. Both are now published together under the title of the first text. See Tsarchen Losal Gyatso, *Celebration of Chinese Tea.*

81 **At Serkhang Monastery of glorious Shalu, all the crazy monks stab with swords**: There must have been some strange clique of eccentric and violent monks at Shalu Monastery for a long time. Sixteen years later, in 1555, Tsarchen's disciple, Jamyang Khyentsé Wangchuk (the fourteenth abbot of Shalu from 1559 until 1568), also mentions the terrifying behavior of the crazy monks (*ban smyon*) at Shalu but speaks respectfully of them and says they requested blessings and were affectionate toward him. See Jamyang Khyentsé Wangchuk, *Marvelous Sheaves*, 153.

87 **Tarpa Monastery** (Thar pa dgon pa): Chal Lotsāwa Chösang (Dpyal Lo tsā ba Chos bzang), the grandson of Chal Kunga Dorjé (Dpyal Kun dga' rdo rje), founded this hermitage in the first decade of the thirteenth century. Other Chal family members were also active there later. The great paṇḍita of Kashmir, Śākyaśrībhadra, visited at the invitation of Chal Lotsāwa (one of his major disciples) and named the monastery. Later, Butön's teacher, the Tibetan translator Tarpa Lotsāwa Nyima Gyaltsen (Thar pa Lo tsā ba Nyi ma rgyal mtshan), who had been abbot of Bodhgayā in India for six years, became the abbot of Tarpa Monastery. Butön spent a total of four years at Tarpa studying Sanskrit grammar and receiving many transmissions of tantric Buddhism from Tarpa Lotsāwa, especially the Six-Branch Yoga and various Kālacakra scriptures and commentaries. See Tāranātha, *Entryway for Experts*, 141–43. Tāranātha also describes many special objects at Tarpa and says one had been brought there from nearby Menlung (Sman lung). Tsarchen does not mention visiting any sacred objects at Tarpa Monastery but notes many at Menlung.

87 **Menlung** (Sman lung): The history of Menlung is also closely associated with the Chal family, which produced a series of tantric masters and translators. Chal Petsa (Dpyal Pe tsa) built the temple at Menlung in the early eleventh century. Later masters of the Chal family, such as Chal Kunga Dorjé, continued to live there in succeeding generations. For a short history of Menlung, see Tāranātha, *Entryway for Experts*, 137–40.

87 **the six ornaments of Nāropa, the Dharma robe of the great paṇḍita of Kashmir, and so forth**: Nāropa (1016–1100) was a major figure in the late tantric Buddhism of India. Many of his teachings came into Tibet in different lineages, especially of the Kagyü tradition.

Śākyaśrībhadra, the great paṇḍita of Kashmir, traveled to Tibet in 1204 and gave many teachings for a period of ten years. See Roerich 1976, 1063–71, for a discussion of Śākyaśrī's life and activities. He granted monastic ordination to many Tibetan monks, and the vinaya transmissions from him continue to the present day. In 1555, sixteen years after Tsarchen's trip, his disciple Jamyang Khyentsé Wangchuk also visited both Tarpa Monastery and Menlung. Khyentsé specifically says "Lord Nāropa's six ornaments" were then kept at Tarpa Monastery, not Menlung, as had been the case when Tsarchen visited. During the intervening years some sacred objects seem to have been moved from Menlung to Tarpa. See Jamyang Khyentsé Wangchuk, *Marvelous Sheaves*, 151, and Tāranātha, *Entryway for Experts*, 143.

87 **the reliquary stūpa of Smṛti** (Smṛi ti'i gdung 'bum): The Indian master Smṛtijñānakīrti lived in Tibet from the late tenth to the early eleventh century. Chal Petsa invited him to Menlung, where he gave many teachings and collaborated on translations of Sanskrit texts into Tibetan. See Tāranātha, *Entryway for Experts*, 137, and, for a detailed account of Smṛti's story, 41–43. Smṛti composed an important Tibetan grammatical text, *Weapon to Open the Door to Speech* (*Smra sgo mtshon cha*), which he is said to have written in Sanskrit and translated into Tibetan himself. It would seem that he passed away at Menlung.

87 **Takshön** (Stag zhon): This form of the Dharma protector Mahākāla, "Mounted on a Tiger," had been a special practice for many generations in Tsarchen's family. See the note on page 151 for more information.

87 **Panam** (Pa rnam): Panam is on the route from Shigatsé to Gyantsé. The region has an ancient history, beginning from the time of the legendary King Gesar (Rgyal po Ge sar) of Ling (Gling). Many Indian masters and their Tibetan students visited and lived in the region during both the early and later spread of Buddhism in Tibet. Tāranātha gives a detailed description of their activities in *Entryway for Experts*, 125–37.

87 **Lhundrup Tsé** (Lhun grub rtse): The grand governor Pakpa Palsang (Nang chen 'Phags pa dpal bzang, 1318–70) founded the Lhundrup Tsé fortress of Panam in 1365. See Jikmé Drakpa, *Rain of Attainments for a Crop of Faith*, 12.

87 **a ruling chieftain sympathetic to the Dharma**: Tsarchen does not mention this man by name, but he was certainly the Panam ruler Gyalwang Dorjé (Pa rnam Sde pa Rgyal dbang rdo rje), who was in power before 1524 and maintained his rule for about another thirty years. See Namkha Palsang, *Downpour of Faith*, 151; Ngawang Tenpai Dorjé, *Enchanting*

Melody of a Divine Drum, 254–55; and Pema Karpo, *Drama of Great Compassion*, 337–440. Gyalwang Dorjé lived to be an old man and had only one daughter. Lacking a male heir, he decided to offer his daughter and the Panam fortress to the Sakya master of the Khön family, Dakchen Kunga Samdrup (Bdag chen Kun dga' bsam 'grub). But the Dakchen realized that many rulers had their eyes on the old man's castle and territory and declined his offer in hope of avoiding a conflict. Gyalwang Dorjé then planned to make the same offer to the ruler of Gyantsé, which severely alarmed other rulers. This unstable situation ignited a series of wars with horrible loss of life, culminating when the armies of the Rinpung ruler seized the Panam fortress. Only with the mediation of the Ngor abbot Könchok Lhundrup was the situation finally calmed and the territorial dispute resolved. Concerning this complicated series of events, which took place in 1555 and 1556, see Jamgön Ameshap, *Ocean of Marvels*, 195–96, and Ngawang Tenpai Dorjé, *Enchanting Melody of a Divine Drum*, 268–69.

87 **a pack ram's leather bag that dashes a fox's daylong hopes**: For example, a fox might see from far away that a leather bag has fallen from the back of a ram that is carrying provisions for a band of nomads. Not realizing that the bag is full of salt, the fox thinks it contains something good to eat. He waits all day for the nomads to leave the area. That night he sneaks to where the bag has been dropped but finds that it is just full of salt, and his daylong hope of something to eat is destroyed. I am grateful to Khenpo Gyatso for explaining this obscure passage.

89 **Samding Monastery** (Bsam sdings dgon pa): This is *not* the famous monastery of the Samding Dorjé Pakmo incarnations near Yamdrok lake. The Samding Monastery that Tsarchen visited in the Panam region of lower Nyang (Nyang smad) was founded by the Shangpa Kagyü master Khedrup Shönu Pal (Mkhas grub Gzhon nu dpal, d. 1319). See Tāranātha, *Entryway for Experts*, 124–25, and Roerich 1976, 749–50. Tsarchen was a lineage holder and practitioner of the Shangpa teachings and is believed to have been both Khyungpo Naljor (Khyung po rnal 'byor, eleventh century) and Sangyé Tönpa (Sangs rgyas ston pa, twelfth–thirteenth centuries) in previous lifetimes.

89 **Potrom protector chapel of the Nigu lineage** (Ni gu brgyud pa'i Pho khrom mgon khang): A chapel of the Dharma protectors of the lineage of the practices transmitted from the Indian yoginī Niguma, which are the core teachings of the Shangpa tradition.

89 **the Dharma lord**: The Dharma lord of Samding Monastery in 1539 was almost certainly the twelfth throne holder, the sovereign adept Sangyé Sengé (Grub thob kyi 'khor lo bsgyur ba

Sangs rgyas seng ge), to whom Tsarchen's teacher Gorumpa would give many initiations and esoteric instructions of the Dharma protectors in 1540, the year after Tsarchen's visit. Sangyé Sengé was said to have mastered the practices of illusory body and dream yoga and to have received direct transmissions from many deities and past masters. See Jamyang Khyentsé Wangchuk, *Rippling Ocean of Wish-Fulfilling Marvels*, 353, 362.

89 **White Protector** (Mgon dkar): A special form of the six-armed Dharma protector Mahākāla originally from the Shangpa tradition. The meditations of the White Protector are often practiced to generate prosperity.

89 **Lhachen Palbar, the protector of Tsi** (Rtsis kyi mgon po Lha chen dpal 'bar): Lhachen Palbar is a special form of the Dharma protector Mahākāla passed down in both the sequential and the treasure transmission lines of the Nyingma tradition.

89 **Tsi Nesar** (Rtsis Gnas gsar): The Tsi Temple (Rtsis Lha khang) in the middle of the Nyang region of Tsang was an ancient place that Guru Padmasambhava blessed. It was believed to be a residence of the Dharma protector Mahākāla. In about the eleventh century, the head of the Asha clan established an estate near the old temple. This new place became known as Nesar (Gnas gsar, "new place"), and so the family there became known as the Tsi Nesarpa (Rtsis Gnas gsar pa). Tsarchen's disciple Jamyang Khyentsé Wangchuk was born at Bodong into the Asha clan, or the Tsi Nesarpa family. See Jamyang Khyentsé Wangchuk, *Marvelous Sheaves*, 9.

89 **the ruler Sönam Rabten** (Sde pa Bsod nams rab brtan): This ruler belonged to the Asha clan of Tsi Nesar. But his relation to the other ruler from the same clan, Namkha Dorjé (the father of Jamyang Khyentsé Wangchuk), is unclear. In the biography of Gorumpa, the Tsi Nesar ruler Sönam Rabten Palsangpo (Bsod nams rab brtan dpal bzang po) is mentioned several times as an important patron. See Jamyang Khyentsé Wangchuk, *Rippling Ocean of Wish-Fulfilling Marvels*, 318, 371, and 393. Curiously, Khyentsé never mentions Sönam Rabten in his autobiography although he was a relative, perhaps even an uncle or a cousin. Khyentsé's father lived at Bodong, but Sönam Rabten apparently lived at the ancestral estate of Nesar.

89 **Dölchung** ('Dol chung): Dölchung is southwest of Panam and west of Tsi Nesar. Tsarchen later mentions Amo Dölchung (A mo 'Dol chung), which may have been the name of the fortress at Dölchung where his niece lived. See Tāranātha, *Entryway for Experts*, 105, for this name in connection with a castle (Ar mo 'Dus chung in the text), and 105–11 for descriptions

of the many ancient places in the Dölchung area and the masters who studied and taught there. Also see Tucci 1989, 67–68. Many spellings are found for this place name, such as Dol 'byung, Mdol 'byung, 'Dul chung, and 'Dus chung.

93 **I might come as a treasure giver**: According to the explanation of Khenpo Gyatso, Tsarchen's niece was hoping that he would come to her place in the role of a treasure discoverer (*gter ston*) of the Nyingma tradition (which he actually was) and give treasure teachings, which could be very lucrative. But Tsarchen saw no point in coming just to contribute to the tax collection of a corrupt local ruler. Could Tsarchen's niece have been the wife of this ruler at Amo Dölchung?

93 **Please don't hope to add oil to fat!**: That is, don't try to needlessly improve something that is already excellent. Tibetans prize the fatty part of meat. According to the explanation of Khenpo Gyatso, Tsarchen is scolding his niece by saying that she should not hope to improve an authentic mendicant yogin (i.e., the fat) by asking him to perform the role of a treasure discoverer (i.e., add oil).

95 **Tri Namkha Sönam** (Khri Nam mkha' bsod nams): This ruler, whom Tsarchen describes as a descendent of the ancient kings of Tibet, had also been a disciple and patron of Kunpang Doringpa. See Tsarchen Losal Gyatso, *Marvels That Cause Body Hairs to Tremble with Faith*, 233. The first syllable of his name is often the first syllable in the names of rulers of Ngari Gungtang (Mnga' ris Gung thang), who were descended from the divine monarchs (*lha btsan po*) of ancient Tibet. But this ruler is not mentioned in their genealogy.

95 **Drongtsé** ('Brong rtse): The two Gyantsé nobles Chenpo Wangyal Pak (Chen po Dbang rgyal 'phags, b. 1375) and his cousin Nangchen Kunga Pak (Nang chen Kun dga' 'phags, 1357–1412), along with Achen Palsang (A chen Dpal bzang), requested from the Chinese Emperor a "mandate from eternal heaven" (*tshe ring gnam gyi she mong*). On the basis of the imperial decree, they founded three fortresses, one of which was Drongtsé, located between Panam and Gyantsé. The other two fortresses were Wangden Tsé (Dbang ldan rtse) at the midpoint of Gyalkhar (Rgyal mkhar) and Norbu Khyungtsé (Nor bu khyung rtse) in the lower valley. See Tāranātha, *Entryway for Experts*, 112–13.

95 **Gyalkhar Tsé** (Rgyal mkhar rtse): The full name for the fortress of Gyantsé in upper Nyang. The grand governor Pakpa Palsang founded it in about 1365. See Jikmé Drakpa, *Rain of Attainments for a Crop of Faith*, 12.

95 **Palkhor Dechen** (Dpal 'khor bde chen): The Dharma king Kunsang Pakpa (Chos rgyal Kun bzang 'phags pa, 1389–1442) founded the monastery of Palkhor Dechen in 1418. He laid the foundation for a massive stūpa in 1427, which was completed in about 1440. For studies of Gyantsé and the great stūpa, see Tucci 1989 and Ricca and Lo Bue 1993.

95 **Gyantsé** (Rgyal rtse): The common abbreviated name for the fortress of Gyalkhar Tsé in upper Nyang.

95 **great ruler** (Sde pa chen mo): The ruler at Gyantsé in 1539 was probably Namkha Lhundrup. He was from the noble family of Latö Lho (La stod Lho) but married into the noble Sharkhapa family at Gyantsé as an adoptive bridegroom (*magpa*). See Everding and Dzongphugpa 2006, 110. (I am grateful to Franz-Karl Ehrhard and Volker Caumanns for this reference.) In the late 1530s or early 1540s, the ruling Dharma king Namkha Lhundrup of the Sharkhapa family (Shar kha Sde srid Chos rgyal Nam mkha' lhun grub, d. ca. 1569) and the Jang (Byang) ruler Namkha Tsewang Dorjé (Nam mkha' tshe dbang rdo rje, d. 1569) combined their armies to defeat the warlord known as Lhasa Dzongpa and invite the exiled Sakya throne holder Ngakchang Kunga Rinchen back to Sakya. See Jamgön Ameshap, *Ocean of Marvels*, 97–99, and 197–98, where the deaths of both rulers are said to have occurred close together. Mangtö Ludrup Gyatso (*Coquette's Mirror*, 446) says the Jang ruler Namkha Tsewang Dorjé (whom he knew well) died in a snake year (*sbrul lo*), soon after he describes the death of Tsarchen in a tiger year (*stag lo*, 1566). The next snake year was 1569.

95 **Drukpa Ngawang Chögyal** ('Brug pa Ngag dbang chos rgyal): Drukpa Ngawang Chögyal (1465–1540) was the fourteenth throne holder of Ralung (Ra lung) Monastery and the head of the Drukpa Kagyü ('Brug pa Bka' brgyud) tradition. The biography of Tsarchen does not mention a previous meeting with Ngawang Chögyal. But it is highly probable that Tsarchen received teachings from the Drukpa master in the late 1520s when he traveled to Ü as the attendant of Dakchen Ngagi Wangchuk. Tsarchen stayed in Ü from about 1524 until the beginning of 1532 and spent part of this time at Nālendra Monastery in Penyul. According to the chronology in the biography of Ngawang Chögyal, the Drukpa master traveled to Penyul between 1527 and 1529, met the Sakya Dakchen there, and gave teachings to his close entourage. Tsarchen would certainly have been included in this group. See Pema Karpo, *Marvel of a Hundred Lights*, 175, 178–79, and 186.

95 **Ralung** (Ra lung): Tsangpa Gyaré Yeshé Dorjé (Gtsang pa Rgya ras Ye shes rdo rje, 1161–1211) established the Drukpa Kagyü tradition and founded the Kagyü monastery of Ralung in

1180. The hereditary leaders of the Drukpa lineage came from his Gya (Rgya) family until the time of the great Pema Karpo (Padma dkar po, 1527–92).

95 **Yamdrok** (Yar 'brog): Yamdrok is a huge lake, near which are the fortress of Nakartsé (Sna dkar rtse) and, somewhat further east, the monastery of Samding (Bsam sdings). This monastery was the seat of the famous Samding Dorjé Pakmo (Bsam sdings Rdo rje phag mo), a series of female teachers believed to be incarnations of the goddess Vajravārāhī. See Dorje 1999, 216–17.

95 **Kharo** (Mkha' ro): Kharo Pass is on the road from Ralung to Nakartsé.

97 **Rongchung** (Rong chung): Rongchung is the valley where the Sakya monastery of Kyetsal in Dreyul ('Bras yul Skyed tshal) is located, which will be the last place described in Tsarchen's journal. See Ferrari 1958, 70, 163, and Dorje 1999, 252.

97 **a young king of Tibet** (Bod rgyal po gzhon nu): Tri Namkha Sönam of Drongtsé (mentioned above), said to be a descendent of the kings of ancient Tibet.

97 **the Shar king** (Shar rgyal po): The previously mentioned Gyantsé ruler, probably the Dharma king Namkha Lhundrup. Tsarchen refers to him as the Shar king because he had married into the Sharkhapa noble family.

97 **my body's feeble leg revealed its own flaw**: For many years, gout or rheumatoid arthritis tormented Tsarchen in one or both of his legs or feet (*zhabs la dreg gis na*). The first mention of the disease in his biography occurs when he is about seventeen years old, and the last mention is here in this travel journal, when he is thirty-eight years old. In 1532, when he was about thirty-one years old and the pain was extremely bad, he had sought relief by placing his legs in the icy waters of the Tsangpo River. Later in the same year, when he was in retreat at Mu (Rmu) and his leg was painful, he wrote to his teacher Ratnabhadra: "My body does not appear at the door of the meditation hut, but the ecstatic primordial awareness in my mind always suppresses [the pain], so I am not depressed." See Ngawang Losang Gyatso, *Sunlight of the Doctrine of the Explication for Disciples*, 499: *bdag kyang lus bsam gtan gyi khang bu'i sgor mi thon kyang sems la bde chen gyi ye shes mnan pas mi non pa khor yug tu yod*. See also 464–65, 485, and 546.

103 **but I was wearied and upset that they were threshing**: Tsarchen was distressed that compulsory laborers were being made to thresh grain. This was considered to be animal's work

and was customarily done by driving cattle over the stalks of grain that had been gathered in a coral. To herd men into a coral and have them do this work was demeaning. I am grateful to Khenpo Gyatso for explaining this passage.

103 **Porok Dodé Gönpo** (Pho rog Mdo sde mgon po): The adept known as Porok Dodé Gönpo, or Jakyungpa (Bya skyungs pa, 1195–1257), was a disciple of Kodrakpa Sönam Gyaltsen (Ko brag pa Bsod nams rgyal mtshan, 1170–1249). See Roerich 1976, 728. The blessed image of Dodé Gönpo that Tsarchen visited was at Jakyung Monastery and held a long-life vase in its hands. The local people would examine the vase and, depending on whether sprouts grew from it in the first month of the Tibetan year (February–March), predict a good or bad harvest for the coming year. See Tāranātha, *Entryway for Experts*, 116.

103 **Namsé Tongmön** (Rnam sras mthong smon): The estate, which Tsarchen had previously visited, of Tri Namkha Sönam, the ruler from Drongtsé.

103 **Menlung Monastery** (Man lung dgon pa): This is *not* the same monastery as the Menlung (Sman lung) that Tsarchen visited earlier in his travels. According to Tāranātha, *Entryway for Experts*, 30–31, 115–16, this ancient monastery was the monastic seat of Drentön Tadral (Bran ston Mtha' bral), who was reborn in his next life as Sönam Pal, the enigmatic Menlung Guru (Man lung Gu ru Bsod nams dpal, b. 1239). The monastery was located in the Taktsé region of Nyang (Myang Stag rtse) and continued to be associated with the hereditary line of Drentön Tadral. It became known as Menlung after Menlung Guru occupied the monastic seat. Menlung Guru traveled twice to India. In 1273 he visited the legendary Śrī Dhānyakaṭaka Stūpa, where the Buddha is said to have first taught the *Kālacakra Tantra*, and then departed as an itinerant yogin (dressed as a *heruka*) bound for the holy site of Potala, never to be heard from again. Menlung Guru composed at least one account of his extensive travels, but none of his writings have yet surfaced. He is also said to have actually visited Shambhala. It is possible that at least part of his account of that journey has survived embedded in another work. See Newman 1996. Also see Roerich 1976, 790–91.

103 **Kharkha** (Mkhar kha): The grand governor Pakpa Palsang founded the fortress of Kharkha in 1365. See Jikmé Drakpa, *Rain of Attainments for a Crop of Faith*, 12.

103 **Taktsal** (Stag tshal): Taktsal is in the upper part of Taktsé in upper Nyang (Myang stod Stag rtse). For a discussion of the Taktsal region, see Tāranātha, *Entryway for Experts*, 113–17.

103 **Shambhar Monastery in Rong** (Rong Sham bhar gyi dgon pa): The Kālacakra master Sherab Sengé (Shes rab seng ge, 1251–1315), son of Ga Lotsāwa Namgyal Dorjé (Rga Lo Rnam rgyal rdo rje, 1203–82), founded Shambhar. Butön studied the Kālacakra at Shambhar under Ga Lotsāwa's grandson, the master Dorjé Gyaltsen (Rdo rje rgyal mtshan, 1283–1325). See Roerich 1976, 792–93.

103 **Dharma lord of Shambhar** (Sham bhar Chos rje): In the following verses and in other texts, Tsarchen usually refers to his teacher as "the wild father" (*pha rgod*). He was apparently from the same clan as Tsarchen. The Fifth Dalai Lama names him as Chökyong Rinchen (Chos skyong rin chen), a mantra bearer of the Dong clan. In the same list, the Great Fifth also describes Tsarchen as a teacher of the Dong clan. See Ngawang Losang Gyatso, *Stream of the River Ganges*, 50b: *mdong gi sngags 'chang drin can pha rgod bla ma chos skyong rin cen/ mdong ston tshar pa chos kyi rgyal po*. (The usual spelling of Tsarchen's clan name is *ldong*, not *mdong*.) In a ritual for offering sacrificial cakes to Takshön, the Tiger-Mounted Protector, Tsarchen quotes several verses his "wild father" wrote, in one of which the master specifically says he had actually seen the body of Takshön. See Tsarchen Losal Gyatso, *Spontaneous Enlightened Action*, 497: *'jigs rung khyod sku mig gis mngon sum mthong*. Before this trip Tsarchen had received from the Shambhar Dharma lord Kunga Sangyé (Sham bhar Chos rje Kun dga' sangs rgyas) the complete initiation and textual transmission of the Nub tradition (Gnub lugs) of Takshön accompanied by many deities. See Ngawang Losang Gyatso, *Sunlight of the Doctrine of the Explication for Disciples*, 489–90.

103 **the protector Takshön** (Mgon po Stag zhon): This form of the Dharma protector Mahākāla "Mounted on a Tiger" was a special guardian of Tsarchen's hereditary line. One night, when Tsarchen was about five years old, his father performed a ritual for Takshön. Tsarchen carried the sacrificial cakes (*gtor ma*) outside to leave them. A terrifying black man actually took the cakes from his hands. Frightened, the boy ran inside and told his father, who said the man was their Dharma protector (i.e., Takshön). See Ngawang Losang Gyatso, *Sunlight of the Doctrine of the Explication for Disciples*, 457. Guru Padmasambhava first taught the Takshön practices in India. Nubchen Sangyé Yeshé (Gnubs chen Sangs rgyas ye shes, b. 832) concealed them as treasures at three locations in Tibet. Dranga Dorjé Kundrak (Drang nga Rdo rje kun grags) finally recovered and translated them. Tsarchen compiled a special volume of texts from the various lineages that spread in Tibet. See Tsarchen Losal Gyatso, *Spontaneous Enlightened Action*, 498; Ngawang Losang Gyatso, *Stream of the River Ganges*, 50a–b; and Ngawang Losang Gyatso, *Sunlight of the Doctrine of the Explication for Disciples*, 549.

103 **the Rongpa Takshön** (Rong pa'i Stag zhon): One of the three locations where Nubchen Sangyé Yeshé concealed the texts of the Takshön tradition in Tibet was in the region of Rong. That specific lineage of the practices is thereby known as the Rongpa. See Tsarchen Losal Gyatso, *Spontaneous Enlightened Action*, 498.

105 **the black Putra who is the henchman of Caturmukha** (Zhal bzhi pa'i las mkhan pu tra nag po): The black Putra, or "black son," is in the retinue of the Dharma protector Caturmukha, a special form of Mahākāla.

105 **Lhanyen Shambhar** (Lha snyan Sham bhar): Probably the name of the mountain where Shambhar Monastery was located.

111 **the ruler's decree from Rinpung**: A decree from Ngawang Namgyal, the ruler of the Rinpung dynasty.

111 **Kyetsal in Dreyul** ('Bras yul Skyed tshal): Jamchen Rabjampa Sangyé Pel (Byams chen rab 'byams pa Sangs rgyas 'phel, 1411–85) founded the Sakya monastery of Kyetsal in 1449. See Ferrari 1958, 70, 163. The Rinpung rulers Norbu Sangpo (Nor bu bzang po, b. 1403) and his son Kunsangpa (Kun bzang pa) were both generous early patrons of Kyetsal Monastery. See Dungkar Losang Trinlé, *Clarification of Knowledge*, 1915–16. One day during his visit to Kyetsal Monastery, Tsarchen stood dressed in saffron robes and a red ceremonial hat and gazed down through a skylight into the main assembly hall. At that moment, Bökharwa Maitri Döndrup Gyaltsen (Bod mkhar ba Mai tri Don grub rgyal mtshan, 1514–75), who would become one of Tsarchen's main disciples, first caught a glimpse of his future master. He had never met Tsarchen before, but just the sight of his face filled him with inexpressible faith. As soon as the assembly was adjourned, Bökharwa met Tsarchen and received an initial blessing from him. For a brief sketch of Bökharwa's life, see Stearns 2006, 261–62.

111 **Lord Dragkar Rabjampa** (Rje Brag dkar Rab 'byams pa): The Sakya master Dragkar Sempa Chenpo Sönam Gyaltsen (Brag dkar sems dpa' chen po Bsod nams rgyal mtshan, d. ca. 1541) was a nephew of Khyenrab Chöjé Rinchen Chokdrup (see note that follows). Dragkar Rabjampa received many teachings from his uncle, from Panchen Shākya Chokden (Paṇ chen Shākya mchog ldan, 1428–1507, who wrote several important works at his request), from Kunpang Doringpa, and from the Kagyü master Treho Chökyi Gyatso. Earlier in his life Tsarchen had requested numerous transmissions from Dragkar Rabjampa, whom he describes as a major upholder of the tradition of Khau Drakzong and as the nephew of Khyenrab Chöjé. Dragkar had eliminated doubts through study and

reflection at Shalu Monastery, gained experience through meditation, and lived as a mendicant hermit. See Tsarchen Losal Gyatso, *Marvels That Cause Body Hairs to Tremble with Faith*, 232. See also Ngawang Losang Gyatso, *Sunlight of the Doctrine of the Explication for Disciples*, 488, 594.

111 **Khyenrab Chöjé** (Mkhyen rab Chos rje): The Sakya master Khyenrab Chöjé Rinchen Chokdrup (Mkhyen rab Chos rje Rin chen mchog grub, 1436–97) was born into the noble Ché (Lce) family at Shalu. After early studies at Shalu, he became a disciple of Ngorchen Kunga Sangpo and Müchen Könchok Gyaltsen (Mus chen Dkon mchog rgyal mtshan, 1388–1469) at Ngor Monastery, and of Dakchen Lodrö Gyaltsen of the Sakya Khön family. Khyenrab Chöjé specialized in tantric teachings such as Kālacakra, Nāro Khecarī, and Rakta Yamāri and was famous as a master of the yoga tantras. At the insistence of Dakchen Lodrö Gyaltsen, he ascended the teaching throne of Nālendra Monastery following a period of serious turmoil and is remembered as the first Chogyé Trichen. For a brief account of Khyenrab Chöjé's life, see Jackson 1989, 27–28.

111 **Khau Drakzongpa** (Kha'u 'brag rdzong pa): A term for the tradition that emanated from Tsarchen's main teacher, Kunpang Doringpa, who lived at the hermitage of Khau Drakzong. The term is basically synonymous with the phrase Explication for Disciples (Slob bshad).

111 **Karmapa Mikyö Dorjé** (Karma pa Mi bskyod rdo rje): The Eighth Karmapa, Mikyö Dorjé (1507–54), was an extremely influential leader of the Kagyü tradition. Many of his scholarly treatises are considered definitive within this lineage. Two of his main Kagyü teachers were Sangyé Nyenpa (Sangs rgyas mnyan pa, 1505–69) and Karma Trinlepa (Karma phrin las pa, 1456–1539).

111 **Rinpung ruler** (Sde pa Rin spungs pa): Ngawang Namgyal (Ngag dbang rnam rgyal, b. 1494?) remained in power until about 1550. At the time of Tsarchen's trip Ngawang Namgyal controlled a large part of Tsang in west-central Tibet. With a group of five hundred horsemen, including his sons, generals, and ministers, he welcomed the Karmapa in Rongchen (Rong chen). With lavish ceremony, including many thousands of monks lining the road and a huge brocade tangka on display, the Karmapa was escorted to Kharu (Mkha' ru), where his encampment was established. The monastic assembly of Kyetsal in Dreyul, including the Dharma lord Jamyang Sarma (Chos rje 'Jam dbyangs gsar ma, d. 1556/57), is specifically mentioned among the thousands of monks who greeted the Karmapa. See Pawo Tsuklak Trengwa, *Feast for Experts*, vol. 2: 1285–86. For a brief summary of Ngawang Namgyal's activities, see Shakabpa, *Political History of Tibet*, vol. 1: 355–56.

113 **Düsum Khyenpa, called Khampa Usé (one of Dakpo Rinpoché's group of chief disciples known as the Three Men of Kham), was the root source of the Karmapas**: The First Karmapa, Düsum Khyenpa (Dus gsum mkhyen pa, 1110–93), or Knower of the Three Times, was also called Khampa Usé (Khams pa Dbu se). After coming from Kham to Ü, he studied widely under teachers of different traditions. In 1139 he met the Kagyü master Dakpo Rinpoché (Dwags po Rin po che), or Gampopa Sönam Rinchen (Sgam po pa Bsod nams rin chen, 1079–1153), from whom he received special Vajrayāna transmissions. From Rechung Dorjé Drak he requested all the teachings of Jetsun Milarepa. In 1189 Düsum Khyenpa founded Tsurpu Monastery, which became the seat of future Karmapa incarnations. See Dungkar Losang Trinlé, *Clarification of Knowledge*, 29–30. The Three Men of Kham (Khams pa mi gsum) were Düsum Khyenpa, Pakmodrupa Dorjé Gyalpo, and Saltong Shogom (Gsal stong sho sgom).

113 **followers of Ganden** (Dga' ldan pa): Ganden is another term for the Geluk tradition that Lord Tsongkhapa Losang Drakpa (Rje Tsong kha pa Blo bzang grags pa, 1357–1419) founded.

115 **the lord, the omniscient Karma Trinlepa** (Rje thams cad mkhyen pa Karma phrin las pa): Lord Karma Trinlepa (1456–1539) was a nephew of the Sakya master Dakpo Panchen Tashi Namgyal (Dwags po Paṇ chen Bkra shis rnam rgyal, 1399–1458), the second abbot of Nālendra Monastery. Karma Trinlepa first practiced medicine as a layman and then took ordination as a Buddhist monk. He studied with masters of all traditions but became particularly expert in the Kagyü and Sakya teachings. He was a major disciple of the Seventh Karmapa, Chödrak Gyatso (Chos grags rgya mtsho, 1454–1506), gained experiential realization through practice of Mahāmudrā and the Six Yogas, and became a lineage holder of these teachings. Later, he was an important teacher of the young Eighth Karmapa. He also bestowed Sakya teachings such as the Lamdré at Nālendra Monastery. See Pawo Tsuklak Trengwa, *Feast for Experts*, vol. 2: 1162–65, and Situ Panchen Chökyi Jungné and Belo Tsewang Kunkhyap, *String of Crystal Gems*, vol. 1: 649–54. Tsarchen had previously received from Karma Trinlepa the Sakya teachings transmitted through Karma Trinlepa's uncle, Tashi Namgyal, such as special instructions on White Tārā, and various teachings of the Kagyü tradition. Immediately after the final events in his travel journal, Tsarchen traveled from Kyetsal Monastery to Nyukla Dzong (Smyug la rdzong), where he visited his old teacher and received the transmission of various protective deities such as Siṃhamukha (Seng gdong can). Tsarchen and Karma Trinlepa were extremely close, and it is said that their minds had blended into one and they could hardly bear to part at the end of this visit, both shedding tears. See Ngawang Losang Gyatso, *Sunlight of the Doctrine of the Explication for Disciples*, 486, 554–55. Karma Trinlepa would pass away just a few months later.

115 **if he was definitely the rebirth of previous Karmapas**: Mikyö Dorjé's recognition as the Eighth Karmapa was disputed for about the first six years of his life. See Rheingans 2010, 268–80.

117 **Karmapa, lord known everywhere as a buddha**: In the autumn of 1974, the Sixteenth Karmapa, Rangjung Rikpai Dorjé (Rang byung rig pa'i rdo rje, 1923–81), visited Vancouver, Canada, during his first trip to North America. Dezhung Rinpoché urged his students in Seattle to go meet him there, telling us many wonderful stories of the Karmapa lineage. Rinpoché had not seen Tsarchen's biography since he had left Tibet fifteen years earlier, but he had memorized this song and would often repeat these opening lines in praise of the Karmapa.

121 **Nairātmyā** (Bdag med ma): The goddess Nairātmyā, the consort of Hevajra, is the source of the Lamdré teachings.

121 **Lord of Yogins** (Rnal 'byor dbang phyug): The great Indian adept Virūpa (seventh–eighth centuries) was the first human recipient of the Lamdré teachings. For the story of Virūpa's life, see Stearns 2006, 138–52. Tsarchen is believed to have been Virūpa in a past lifetime.

121 **a Dharma such as this**: That is, the special Lamdré teachings in the tradition of the Explication for Disciples.

BIBLIOGRAPHY

Tibetan Sources

Chökyi Gyatso, Katok Situ (Chos kyi rgya mtsho, Kaḥ thog Si tu). *Necklace of Moon Crystals: A Travelogue of Pilgrimage in Ü and Tsang. Gangs ljongs dbus gtsang gnas bskor lam yig nor bu zla shel gyi se mo do*. Tashijong: Sungrab Nyamso Gyunphel Parkhang, 1972.

Darpa Rinchen Palsang ('Dar pa Rin chen dpal bzang). *Rippling Ocean of Blessed Nectar. Byin rlabs bdud rtsi'i chu gter rgod pa*. Biographical supplication of fifty-one quatrains extracted from the Fifth Dalai Lama's biography of Tsarchen.

Dungkar Losang Trinlé (Dung dkar Blo bzang 'phrin las). *Clarification of Knowledge: The Great Lexicon of Tibetology. Mkhas dbang dung dkar blo bzang 'phrin las mchog gis mdzad pa'i bod rig pa'i tshig mdzod chen mo shes bya rab gsal*. Beijing: China Tibetology Publishing House, 2002.

Jamgön Ameshap Ngawang Kunga Sönam ('Jam mgon A mes zhabs Ngag dbang kun dga' bsod nams). *A Sun Illuminating All the Teachings of the Dharma Protectors: The History of the Profound Dharma Cycles of Mahākāla. Dpal rdo rje nag po chen po'i zab mo'i chos skor rnams byung ba'i tshul legs par bshad pa bstan srung chos kun gsal ba'i nyin byed.* 2 vols. New Delhi: T. G. Dhongthog Rinpoche, 1979.

_____. *Fulfillment of All Needs and Wishes: A Treasury of Marvelous Jewels, the Biographies of the Precious Hereditary Lineage of the Glorious Sakyapa, the Great Heirs of the Buddha in the Northern Regions of Jambudvīpa. 'Dzam gling byang phyogs kyi thub pa'i rgyal tshab chen po dpal ldan sa skya pa'i gdung rabs rin po che ji ltar byon pa'i tshul gyi rnam par thar pa ngo mtshar rin po che'i bang mdzod dgos 'dod kun 'byung*. Delhi: Tashi Dorji, 1975.

_____. *Ocean of Marvels: A Biography of Ngakchang Kunga Rinchen. Srid pa gsum gyi bla ma dpal sa skya pa chen po sngags 'chang ngag gi dbang po kun dga' rin chen gyi rnam par thar pa ngo mtshar rgya mtsho*. Delhi: T. G. Dhongthog Rinpoche, 1980.

Jampai Pal, Tropu Lotsāwa (Byams pa'i dpal, Khro phu Lo tsā ba). *Wish-Fulfilling Vine: The Autobiography of Tropu Lotsāwa. Khro lo chen pos mdzad pa'i dpag bsam 'khri shing. Dbu med* ms., 90 fols. Beijing: Cultural Palace of Nationalities.

Jamyang Khyentsé Wangchuk ('Jam dbyangs mkhyen brtse'i dbang phyug). *Marvelous Sheaves: The Autobiography of Jamyang Khyentsé Wangchuk. Bla ma rin po che mkhan chen pa'i rnam thar ngo mtshar snye ma zhes bya ba sgro bkur dang bral zhing yid ches la dgod bro ba zhig.* In *Sa-skya Lam-'bras Literature Series*, vol. 3: 1–250. Dehra Dun: Sakya Centre, 1983.

______. *Rippling Ocean of Wish-Fulfilling Marvels: A Biography of Gorumpa Kunga Lekpa. Rje btsun rdo rje 'chang sgo rum pa chen po kun dga' legs pa'i blo gros rgyal mtshan dpal bzang po'i rigs sngags kyi rtogs pa brjod pa'i gtam ngo mtshar yid bzhin gyi chu gter bzhad pa.* In *Sa-skya Lam-'bras Literature Series*, vol. 2: 249–397. Dehra Dun: Sakya Centre, 1983.

Jikmé Drakpa ('Jigs med grags pa). *Rain of Attainments for a Crop of Faith: A Biography of the Dharma King of Gyantsé. Rgyal rtse chos rgyal gyi rnam par thar pa dad pa'i lo thog dngos grub kyi char 'bebs.* Lhasa: Bod ljongs mi dmangs dpe skrun khang, 1987.

Khyenrab Jampa Ngawang Lhundrup (Mkhyen rab byams pa Ngag dbang lhun grub). *Fine Vase of Blessed Nectar: A Brief Biography of Tsarchen Losal Gyatso. Slob bshad bstan pa'i shing rta ba chen po tshar chen rdo rje 'chang blo gsal rgya mtsho grags pa rgyal mtshan dpal bzang po'i rnam thar mdor bsdus byin rlabs bdud rtsi'i bum bzang.* In *'Jam dbyangs tshar chen chos kyi rgyal po'i rnam thar sogs mgur tshan* (7 fols.), ff. 1a–5b. St. Petersburg: The State Hermitage.

Kunga Drölchok, Jetsun (Kun dga' grol mchog, Rje btsun). *A Travel Journal to Dispel Darkness from the Heart of a Discerning Person. Lam yig dpyod ldan snying gi mun sel. Dbu med* ms., 44 fols. Beijing: Cultural Palace of Nationalities.

______. *Amazing Ornament to My Autobiography. Rnam thar mtshar rgyan.* In *Rje btsun kun dga' grol mchog gi phyi nang gsang gsum gyi rnam thar*, 288–319. Beijing: Mi rigs dpe skrun khang, 2005.

Lodrö Gyaltsen, Sokdokpa (Blo gros rgyal mtshan, Sog zlog pa). *Dragon Roar of Scripture and Reasoning: A Reply to Karmapa Mikyö Dorjé's Questions Concerning the Nyingma Tradition. Rgyal ba'i dbang po karma pa mi bskyod rdo rjes gsang sngags rnying ma rnams la dri ba'i chab shog gnang ba'i dris lan lung dang rigs pa'i 'brug sgra.* In *Ngagyur Nyingmay Sungrab*, vol. 2: 1–173. Gangtok: Sonam Kazi, 1971.

Mangtö Ludrup Gyatso (Mang thos klu sgrub rgya mtsho). *Coquette's Mirror: The Autobiography of Mangtö Ludrup Gyatso. Rang gi rnam par thar pa yul sna tshogs kyi bdud rtsi myong ba'i gtam du byas pa zol zog rdzun gyis ma bslad pa sgeg mo'i me long.* In *Sa-skya Lam-'bras Literature Series*, vol. 3: pp. 395–625. Dehra Dun: Sakya Centre, 1983.

Namkha Palsang (Nam mkha' dpal bzang). *Downpour of Faith: A Biography of Lhachok Sengé. Dpal ldan bla ma dam pa rgyal ba lha mchog seng ge'i rnam thar dad pa'i char 'bebs.* In *Gsung ngag lam 'bras tshogs bshad chen mo*, vol. 28: 125–72. Kathmandu: Sa skya rgyal yongs gsung rab slob gnyer khang, 2008.

Ngawang Losang Gyatso, Dalai Lama (Ngag dbang blo bzang rgya mtsho, Tā la'i bla ma). *Divine Fabric of Transparency: The Autobiography of the Fifth Dalai Lama. Za hor gyi ban de ngag dbang blo bzang rgya mtsho'i 'di snang 'khrul ba'i rol rtsed rtogs brjod kyi tshul du bkod pa du kū la'i gos bzang las glegs bam dang po*. Lhasa: Bod ljongs mi dmangs dpe skrun khang, 1989.

_____. *Stream of the River Ganges: A Record of Teachings Received. Zab pa dang rgya che ba'i dam pa'i chos kyi thob yig ganggā'i chu rgyun las glegs bam gsum pa*. Delhi: Nechung and Lakhar, 1971.

_____. *Sunlight of the Doctrine of the Explication for Disciples: A Biography of Tsarchen Losal Gyatso. Rigs dang dkyil 'khor kun gyi khyab bdag rdo rje 'chang blo gsal rgya mtsho grags pa rgyal mtshan dpal bzang po'i rnam par thar pa slob bshad bstan pa'i nyi 'od*. In *Sa-skya Lam-'bras Literature Series*, vol. 2: 399–637. Dehra Dun: Sakya Centre, 1983. With few spelling differences, this version seems to have been copied directly from the earlier Lhasa edition of the same title in volume 9 (TA), pp. 371–610, of *Thams cad mkhyen pa rgyal ba lnga pa chen po ngag dbang blo bzang rgya mtsho'i gsung 'bum, The Collected Works (Gsung 'bum) of the Vth Dalai Lama Ngag-dbang blo-bzang rgya-mtsho*, Gangtok, Sikkim: Sikkim Research Institute of Tibetology, 1991–95.

Ngawang Losang Tenpai Gyaltsen (Ngag dbang blo bzang bstan pa'i rgyal mtshan). *Illuminating the Marvels: Biographies of the Lineal Masters of Glorious Hayagrīva as Yangsang Tröpa. Dpal chen rta mgrin yang gsang khros pa'i dbang gi bla ma brgyud pa'i rnam par thar pa mdo tsam brjod pa dad pa'i spu long g.yo byed ngo mtshar snang ba*. In *The Collected Works of Lcang-lung Paṇḍi-ta Ngag-dbang blo-bzang bstan-pa'i rgyal-mtshan*, vol. 2: 185–337. Delhi: Mongolian Lama Gurudeva, 1975–85.

Ngawang Tenpai Dorjé (Ngag dbang brtan pa'i rdo rje). *Enchanting Melody of a Divine Drum: A Biography of Ngorchen Könchok Lhundrup. Rje btsun bla ma dam pa ngor chen thams cad mkhyen pa dkon mchog lhun grub kyi rnam par thar pa rab snyan lha'i rnga dbyangs*. In *Gsung ngag lam 'bras tshogs bshad chen mo*, vol. 28: 233–85. Kathmandu: Sa skya rgyal yongs gsung rab slob gnyer khang, 2008.

Ngorchen Kunga Sangpo (Ngor chen Kun dga' bzang po). *Oceanic Record of Teachings Received. Thob yig rgya mtsho*. In *The Complete Works of the Great Masters of the Sa skya Sect of Tibetan Buddhism (Sa skya pa'i bka' 'bum)*, vol. 9: 44.4–108.4. Tokyo: The Toyo Bunko, 1968.

Pawo Tsuklak Trengwa (Dpa' bo Gtsug lag phreng ba). *Feast for Experts: A History of Dharma. Chos byung mkhas pa'i dga' ston*. 2 vols. Beijing: Mi rigs dpe skrun khang, 1986.

Pema Karpo, Kunkhyen (Padma dkar po, Kun mkhyen). *Drama of Great Compassion: The Autobiography of Pema Karpo. Sems dpa' chen po padma dkar po'i rnam thar thugs rje chen po'i zlos gar*. In *Collected Works (Gsung 'bum) of Kun-mkhyen Padma dkar-po*, vol. 3: 339–597. Darjeeling: Kargyud Sungrab Nyamso Khang, 1973–74.

_____. *Marvel of a Hundred Lights: A Biography of Ngawang Chögyal. Dpal ldan bla ma dam pa ngag dbang chos kyi rgyal po'i rnam par thar pa ngo mtshar 'od brgya pa*. In *Collected Works (Gsung 'bum) of Kun-mkhyen Padma dkar-po*, vol. 3: 111–219. Darjeeling: Kargyud Sungrab Nyamso Khang, 1973–1974.

Shakabpa, W. D. (Zhwa sgab pa Dbang phyug bde ldan). *Political History of Tibet. Bod kyi srid don rgyal rabs*. 2 vols. Delhi: Tsepal Taikhang, 1976.

Situ Panchen Chökyi Jungné (Si tu Paṇ chen Chos kyi 'byung gnas) and Belo Tsewang Kunkhyap ('Be lo Tshe dbang kun khyab). *String of Crystal Gems: A History of the Karma Kamtsang Tradition. Bsgrub brgyud karma kam tshang brgyud pa rin po che'i ram par thar pa rab 'byams nor bu zla ba chu shel gyi phreng ba*. 2 vols. New Delhi: D. Gyaltsan and K. Legshay, 1972.

Sönam Drakpa, Panchen (Bsod nams grags pa, Paṇ chen). *Magical Key to Royal Genealogies, or Red Annals, or New Annals. Rgyal rabs 'phrul gyi lde mig gam deb ther dmar po 'am deb gsar ma*. Lhasa: Bod ljongs mi dmangs dpe skrun khang, 1982.

Tāranātha, Jonang (Tā ra nā tha, Jo nang). *Entryway for Experts: A History of the Nyang Region. Myang yul stod smad bar gsum gyi ngo mtshar gtam gyi legs bshad mkhas pa'i 'jug ngogs*. Lhasa: Bod ljongs mi dmangs dpe skrun khang, 1983.

Tsarchen Losal Gyatso (Tshar chen Blo gsal rgya mtsho). *Ballad of the Cuckoo: My Autobiographical Song of the Road. Rang gi rtogs pa brjod pa lam glu dpyid kyi rgyal mo'i glu dbyangs. Dbu med* ms., 17 fols. Published as an *dbu can* text (with many editorial changes) in *Many Other Teachings. Sna tshogs pod*, vol. *kha*: 107–36. Kathmandu: Sa skya rgyal yongs gsung rab slob gnyer khang, 2007.

_____. *Celebration of Blooming White Lotuses: A Supplication to the Lineage of Nāro Khecarī. Nā ro mkha' spyod ma'i brgyud pa'i gsol ba 'debs pa pad dkar bzhad pa'i dga' ston*. In *Many Other Teachings. Sna tshogs pod*, vol. *kha*: 325–30. Kathmandu: Sa skya rgyal yongs gsung rab slob gnyer khang, 2007.

_____. *Celebration of Chinese Tea. Ja mchod rgya ja'i chu gter rba rlabs g.yo ba'i dga' ston*. In *Many Other Teachings. Sna tshogs pod*, vol. *kha*: 463–67. Kathmandu: Sa skya rgyal yongs gsung rab slob gnyer khang, 2007.

_____. *Garland of Captivating Water Lilies: A Biography of Dakchen Lodrö Gyaltsen. Khams gsum chos kyi rgyal po bdag chen rdo rje 'chang blo gros rgyal mtshan dpal bzang po'i rnam par thar pa yid 'phrog utpa la'i do shal*. In *Sa-skya Lam-'bras Literature Series*, vol. 2: 35–151. Dehra Dun: Sakya Centre, 1983.

_____. *Marvels That Cause Body Hairs to Tremble with Faith: A Biography of Kunpang Doringpa. Dpal ldan bla ma dam pa kun spangs chos kyi rgyal po'i rnam par thar pa ngo mtshar dad pa'i spu long g.yo ba*. In *Sa-skya Lam-'bras Literature Series*, vol. 2: 153–247. Dehra Dun: Sakya Centre, 1983.

_____. *Quick Bestower of Attainments: A Method for Realization of Yangsang Tröpa. Bcom ldan 'das yang gsang khros pa yab yum rkyang sgrub kyi sgrub thabs rgyun khyer dngos grub myur stsol*. In *Many Other Teachings. Sna tshogs pod*, vol. *kha*: 269–82. Kathmandu: Sa skya rgyal yongs gsung rab slob gnyer khang, 2007.

_____. *Radiant Light Illuminating the Fine Path: Collected Songs of an Expert and Revered Accomplished Master, the Venerable Lord Losal Gyatso. Mkhas btsun grub pa'i dbang phyug rje btsun blo gsal rgya mtsho'i mgur 'bum gyi tshogs lam bzang gsal ba'i 'od snang.* In *Many Other Teachings. Sna tshogs pod*, vol. *kha*: 163–200. Kathmandu: Sa skya rgyal yongs gsung rab slob gnyer khang, 2007.

_____. *Realized Expert of the North: A Biographical Supplication to the Great Gorumpa. Rdo rje 'chang sgo rum pa chen po'i rnam thar gsol 'debs byang phyogs mkhas grub ma. Sna tshogs pod*, vol. *kha*: 153–58. Kathmandu: Sa skya rgyal yongs gsung rab slob gnyer khang, 2007.

_____. *Sealed Secret Autobiography. Gsang ba'i rnam thar bka' rgya ma.* In *Many Other Teachings. Sna tshogs pod*, vol. *kha*: 201–5. Kathmandu: Sa skya rgyal yongs gsung rab slob gnyer khang, 2007.

_____. *Spontaneous Enlightened Action: A Ritual for Offering Sacrificial Cakes to the Protector Takshön. Mgon po stag zhon snubs lugs kyi gtor chog 'phrin las lhun grub.* In *Many Other Teachings. Sna tshogs pod*, vol. *kha*: 469–98. Kathmandu: Sa skya rgyal yongs gsung rab slob gnyer khang, 2007.

_____. *Supplication to the Masters of the Precious Teaching. Gsung ngag rin po che brgyud pa gsum 'dus kyi bla ma la gsol ba 'debs pa lam rim smon lam dang bcas pa.* In *Sa-skya Lam-'bras Literature Series*, vol. 14: 235–48. Dehra Dun: Sakya Centre, 1983.

_____. *Supplication to the Venerable Lord for Whom Confusion Has Vanished. Rje btsun 'khrul zhig ka bzhi pa'i zhal snga nas la gsol 'debs.* In *Many Other Teachings. Sna tshogs pod*, vol. *kha*: 159–62. Kathmandu: Sa skya rgyal yongs gsung rab slob gnyer khang, 2007.

Yarlungpa Abum (Yar lung pa A 'bum). *Rough Genealogy of the Rinpung Dynasty. Dpal ldan rin chen spungs pa sger gyi gdung rabs che long tsam zhig.* In *Sngon gyi gtam me tog gi phreng ba*, 125–34. Incomplete *dbu med* manuscript. Dharamsala: Library of Tibetan Works and Archives, 1985.

Sources in European Languages

Dorje, Gyurme. 1999. *Tibet Handbook.* Bath: Footprint Books.

Essen, Gerd-Wolfgang, and Tsering Tashi Thingo. 1989. *Die Götter des Himalaya: Buddhistische Kunst Tibets: Die Sammlung Gerd-Wolfgang Essen.* 2 vols. Munich: Prestel-Verlag.

Everding, Karl-Heinz, and Dawa Dargyay Dzongphugpa. 2006. *Das tibetische Fürstentum La stod lHo (um 1265–1642): Die Geschichte der Herrschaftsbildung nebst einer Edition der Chronik Shel dkar chos 'byung.* Wiesbaden: Dr. Ludwig Reichert Verlag.

Ferrari, Alfonsa. 1958. *mKhyen-brtse's Guide to the Holy Places of Central Tibet.* Rome: Istituto Italiano per il Medio ed Estremo Oriente.

Jackson, David. 1989. *The Early Abbots of 'Phan-po Na-lendra: The Vicissitudes of a Great Tibetan Monastery in the 15th Century.* Vienna: Arbeitskreis für Tibetische und Buddhistische Studien, Universität Wien.

Karmay, Samten Gyaltsen. 1988. *The Great Perfection (Rdzogs chen): A Philosophical and Meditative Teaching in Tibetan Buddhism.* Leiden: E. J. Brill.

Matsuo, Bashō. 1991. *Narrow Road to the Interior*. Translated by Sam Hamill. Boston and London: Shambhala Publications.

Merwin, W. S. 2008. *The Shadow of Sirius*. Port Townsend WA: Copper Canyon Press.

Newman, John. 1996. "Itineraries to Sambhala." In *Tibetan Literature: Studies in Genre*, edited by José Ignacio Cabezón and Roger R. Jackson, 485–99. Ithaca: Snow Lion Publications.

Ngor Thartse Khenpo Sonam Gyatso (ngor thar rtse mkhan po bsod nams rgya mtsho). 1983. *Seizō "mandara" shūsei: Chibetto Mandara. Tibetan Mandalas: The Ngor Collection*. 2 vols. Tokyo: Kodansha International.

Petech, Luciano. 1990. *Central Tibet and the Mongols*. Rome: Istituto Italiano per il Medio ed Estremo Oriente.

Rheingans, Jim. 2010. "Narratives of Reincarnation, Politics of Power, and the Emergence of a Scholar: The Very Early Years of Mikyö Dorje." In *Lives Lived, Lives Imagined: Biography in the Buddhist Traditions*, edited by Linda Covill, Ulrike Roesler, and Sarah Shaw, 241–97. Boston: Wisdom Publications.

Ricca, Franco, and Erberto Lo Bue. 1993. *The Great Stupa of Gyantse*. London: Serindia Publications.

Richardson, Hugh. 1998. *High Peaks, Pure Earth: Collected Writings on Tibetan History and Culture*. London: Serindia Publications.

Roerich, George N., trans. 1976. *The Blue Annals*. Delhi: Motilal Banarsidass.

Schäfer, Ernst. 1943. *Geheimnis Tibet: Erster Bericht der Deutschen Tibet-Expedition Ernst Schäfer*. Munich: Bruckmann.

Seyfort Ruegg, David. 1966. *The Life of Bu ston rin po che*. Rome: Istituto Italiano per il Medio ed Estremo Oriente.

Stearns, Cyrus. 2001. *Luminous Lives: The Story of the Early Masters of the Lam 'bras Tradition in Tibet*. Boston: Wisdom Publications.

_____, trans. 2006. *Taking the Result as the Path: Core Teachings of the Sakya Lamdré Tradition*. Boston: Wisdom Publications.

_____. 2010. *The Buddha from Dölpo: A Study of the Life and Thought of the Tibetan Master Dölpopa Sherab Gyaltsen*. Ithaca: Snow Lion Publications.

Tucci, Giuseppe. 1949. *Tibetan Painted Scrolls*. 3 vols. Rome: La Libreria dello Stato. Reprint, 1999, Bangkok: SDI Publications.

_____. 1973. *Transhimalaya*. Geneva: Nagel Publishers.

_____. 1989. *Gyantse and Its Monasteries: Part I* [English translation of *Indo-Tibetica IV.1* by Uma Marini Vesci]. New Delhi: Aditya Prakashan.

INDEX

A

Abhayākaragupta, 141
Achen Palsang (A chen Dpal bzang), 147
Amdo (A mdo), 140
Amitāyus, 47, 131
Amo Dölchung (A mo 'Dol chung). *See* Dölchung
Asha ('A zhwa) clan, 130–31, 146
Atiśa, 16
Avalokiteśvara, 67, 135
Avalokiteśvara Khasarpaṇa, 141

B

Bektsé (Beg tse), 128–29
Bloody Mount Sinpo (Khrag 'dzag Srin po'i ri), 55, 133
Bodhgayā, 143
Bodong (Bo dong), 8–9, 13, 47, 130–32, 146
Bodong Panchen Choklé Namgyal (Bo dong Paṇ chen Phyogs las rnam rgyal, 1376–1451), 130
Bodong Rinchen Tsemo (Bo dong Rin chen rtse mo), 127
Bökharwa Maitri Döndrup Gyaltsen (Bod mkhar ba Mai tri Don grub rgyal mtshan, 1514–75), 15, 152
Buddha Śākyamuni, 33, 75, 126, 136–37
Buddhaguhya, 138
Butön Rinchen Drup (Bu ston Rin chen grub, 1290–1364), 15, 77–79, 139, 141, 143, 151

C

Cakrasamvara, 133
Caturmukha, 105, 138, 152
Chakgok Valley (Lcags sgog lung), 142
Chaktang (Lcags thang), 39
Chaktö (Lcags stod), 73, 139
Chal (Dpyal) family, 143
Chal Kunga Dorjé (Dpyal Kun dga' rdo rje), 143
Chal Lotsāwa Chösang (Dpyal Lo tsā ba Chos bzang), 143
Chal Petsa (Dpyal Pe tsa), 143–44
Ché (Lce) family, 153
Chenpo Wangyal Pak (Chen po Dbang rgyal 'phags, b. 1375), 147

Chetsun Sherab Jungné (Lce btsun Shes rab 'byung gnas), 139–41
Chödrak Gyatso (Chos grags rgya mtsho, 1454–1506), 154
Chogyé abbot (Bco brgyad pa). *See* Chogyé Trichen
Chogyé Trichen (Bco brgyad khri chen), 77, 141–42, 153
Chogyé Trichen Rinpoché (Bco brgyad khri chen Rin po che, 1919–2007), 143
Chökhor Yangtsé (Chos 'khor yang rtse), 18
Chökyong Rinchen (Chos skyong rin chen), 151
Chöying Dorjé (Chos dbyings rdo rje, 1604–74), 19–20
Chukpo Sharpa (Phyug po Shar pa), 39
Chumik Ringmo (Chu mig ring mo), 9, 68, 71, 137–38
Chumolung Monastery (Chu mo lung gi dgon pa), 8, 45, 129

D

Dakchen Chumikpa Lodrö Wangchuk (Bdag chen Chu mig pa Blo gros dbang phyug, 1402–81), 137
Dakchen Kunga Samdrup (Bdag chen Kun dga' bsam 'grub), 145
Dakchen Lodrö Gyaltsen (Bdag chen Blo gros rgyal mtshan, 1444–95), 17, 19, 49, 126, 130–31, 133, 153
Dakchen Ngagi Wangchuk (Bdag chen Ngag gi dbang phyug, d. 1544), 3, 29, 124–25
Dakchen Rinpoché (Bdag chen Rin po che). *See* Ngakchang Kunga Rinchen
Dakchen Rinpoché Draklopa (Bdag chen Rin po che Grags blo pa, 1367–1437 or 1446), 71, 138
Dakpo Panchen Tashi Namgyal (Dwags po Paṇ chen Bkra shis rnam rgyal, 1399–1458), 154
Dakpo Rinpoché (Dwags po Rin po che). *See* Gampopa Sönam Rinchen
Dampa Marpo (Dam pa dmar po), 67, 135
Dar ('Dar), 15, 20, 27, 33, 77, 124, 126
Darchar Rinchen Sangpo ('Dar phyar Rin chen bzang po), 127–29
Darpa Rinchen Palsang ('Dar pa Rin chen dpal bzang), 5, 15, 18, 126
Darpa Sönam Lhundrup ('Dar pa Bsod nams lhun grub), 18
Dezhung Rinpoché (Sde gzhung Rin po che, 1906–87), 19, 21, 142–43, 155
Dhānyakaṭaka Stūpa, Śrī, 150
Dharmakīrti, 131
Dölchung ('Dol chung), 89, 93, 146–47
Dölpopa Sherab Gyaltsen (Dol po pa Shes rab rgyal mtshan, 1292–1361), 8, 127
Döndrup Ling (Don 'grub gling), 35
Dong (Ldong/Mdong) clan, 151
Donga (Gdong dga'), 15
Dönyö Dorjé (Don yod rdo rje, 1463–1512), 136
Dori (Do ri), 97
Doring Kunpangpa (Rdo ring Kun spangs pa). *See* Kunpang Doringpa
Doringpa (Rdo ring pa). *See* Kunpang Doringpa
Dorjé Gyaltsen (Rdo rje rgyal mtshan, 1283–1325), 151
Dorjé Rabtenma (Rdo rje rab brtan ma), 79, 140–42

Dragkar Rabjampa (Brag dkar Rab 'byams pa). *See* Dragkar Sempa Chenpo Sönam Gyaltsen
Dragkar Sempa Chenpo Sönam Gyaltsen (Brag dkar sems dpa' chen po Bsod nams rgyal mtshan, d. 1541?), 12, 111, 152–53
Drakgowa (Brag sgo ba), 79, 85
Drakpa Lodrö (Grags pa blo gros). *See* Dakchen Rinpoché Draklopa
Drakram Abbey (Brag ram Chos sde), 45, 127–28
Dranga Dorjé Kundrak (Drang nga Rdo rje kun grags), 151
Drentön Tadral (Bran ston Mtha' bral), 150
Dreyul ('Bras yul), 111–13, 149, 152–53
Drokmi Lotsāwa ('Brog mi Lo tsā ba, 993–1077?), 138
Drongtsé ('Brong rtse), 95, 147, 150
Drukpa Kagyü ('Brug pa Bka' brgyud), 11, 148
Drukpa Ngawang Chögyal ('Brug pa Ngag dbang chos rgyal, 1465–1540), 11, 95–97, 148
Drüm (Grum), 29, 124
Drung Gyalwa (Drung Rgyal ba), 77
Drungchen (Drung chen), 77
Düsum Khyenpa / Khampa Usé (Dus gsum mkhyen pa / Khams pa Dbu se, 1110–93), 113, 154
Dzilung (Rdzi lung), 51
Dzingpu (Rdzi phu), 79

E

Enshrī Gyalwa Kuntu Sangpo (Dben shrī Rgyal ba kun tu bzang po), 139–40
Enshrī Gyalwa Sangpo (Dben shrī Rgyal ba bzang po), 73, 139–40
Enshrī Shākya Sangpo (Dben shrī Shākya bzang po), 139–140
Explication for Disciples. *See* Lobshé

F

Face-Viewing Temple (Zhal ras lha khang), 53, 59, 133
Fifth Dalai Lama, Ngawang Losang Gyatso (Tā la'i bla ma Ngag dbang blo bzang rgya mtsho, 1617–82), 4, 17, 20, 125–26
  biography of Tsarchen, 5, 15, 17–18, 125, 134, 141–42, 151
five emissaries (Ging lnga), 45, 129

G

Ga Lotsāwa Namgyal Dorjé (Rga Lo Rnam rgyal rdo rje, 1203–82), 151
Gampopa Sönam Rinchen (Sgam po pa Bsod nams rin chen, 1079–1153), 113, 154
Ganden (Dga' ldan), 113, 154
Gangchen Chöpel Monastery (Gangs can chos 'phel gyi dgon pa), 67, 135–36
Gatön Ngawang Lekpa Rinpoché (Sga ston Ngag dbang legs pa Rin po che, 1864–1941), 19, 130
Gawadong (Dga' ba gdong), 124
Geding (Dge sdings), 9–10, 53, 59–61, 132–33
Geluk (Dge lugs), 135, 154
Gesar, King (Rgyal po Ge sar), 144
Gongma Kunga Lodrö (Gong ma Kun dga' blo gros, 1729–83), 21
Göngyo (Gon gyo), 140

Gorumpa Kunga Lekpa (Sgo rum pa Kun dga' legs pa, 1477–1544), 9, 13, 47–51, 127, 130–32, 146
Gu Pass (Gu la), 103
Gya (Rgya) family, 149
Gyagar Sherab Gyaltsen (Rgya gar Shes rab rgyal mtshan, 1436–94), 19, 132
Gyalkhar Tsé, 95, 147 (Rgyal mkhar rtse). *See also* Gyantsé
Gyaltsa Rinchen Gön (Rgyal tsha Rin chen mgon), 133
Gyalwang Dorjé (Rgyal dbang rdo rje), 144–45
Gyantsé (Rgyal rtse), 11, 95, 144–45, 147–48
great stūpa of, 11–12, 95, 148
Gyengong Temple (Rgyan gong), 77, 85, 140

H

Hayagrīva, 8, 18, 79, 128–29, 135. *See also* Pema Wangchen Yangsang Tröpa
Hevajra, 47, 130, 133, 155
Horché Töntsul (Hor che Ston tshul), 140
Hushrī Göpo Rinchen (Hu shrī Rgod po rin chen), 73, 140

J

Jakyung Monastery (Bya skyungs), 150
Jakyungpa (Bya skyungs pa). *See* Porok Dodé Gönpo
Jamgön Ameshap ('Jam mgon A mes zhabs, 1597–1659), 20
Jamyang Gawai Shenyen ('Jam dbyangs dga' ba'i bshes gnyen), 18
Jamyang Khyentsé Wangchuk ('Jam dbyangs mkhyen brtse'i dbang phyug, 1524–68), 14–15, 130–31, 134, 139, 143–44, 146
Jamyang Kunga Sönam Drakpa Gyaltsen / Salo Jampai Dorjé ('Jam dbyangs kun dga' bsod nams grags pa rgyal mtshan / Sa Lo 'Jam pa'i rdo rje). *See* Sakya Lotsāwa
Jamyang Sarma ('Jam dbyangs gsar ma, d. 1556/57), 153
Jang (Byang), 132, 148
Jingim (Jim Gyim), 137
Jñānaśrī, 137
Jolepa (Jo las pa), 77
Jomonang (Jo mo nang). *See* Jonang
Jonang (Jo nang), 8–9, 13–14, 19, 41, 127, 131–32
great stūpa of, 7–8, 41, 127

K

Kagyü (Bka' brgyud), 2, 7, 11, 13, 77, 128, 131, 133, 136, 141, 143, 148, 152–54
Kālacakra, 128, 130, 132, 143, 151, 153
Kālacakra Tantra, 127, 150
Karma Trinlepa (Karma phrin las pa, 1456–1539), 13, 115, 153–54
Karmapa (Karma pa). *See* Chödrak Gyatso; Chöying Dorjé; Düsum Khyenpa; Mikyö Dorjé; Rangjung Rikpai Dorjé
Kham (Khams), 19, 79, 140, 154
Three Men of (Khams pa mi gsum), 113, 154
Kharkha (Mkhar kha), 103, 150
Kharo (Mkha' ro), 95, 149
Kharu (Mkha' ru), 153
Khau cliffs (Kha'u brag), 29, 121, 124
Khau Drakzong (Kha'u brag rdzong), 2–3, 37, 124, 135, 152–53
Khau Drakzongpa (Kha'u brag rdzong pa), 111, 153

Khecara (Mkha' spyod), 15–16, 59, 65, 134
Khecarī (Mkha' spyod ma), 2, 59, 134–35. *See also* Nāro Khecarī; Vajrayoginī; Vārāhī
Khedrup Shönu Pal (Mkhas grub Gzhon nu dpal, d. 1319), 145
Khenchen Appey Rinpoché (Mkhan chen A pad Rin po che, 1927–2010), 133
Khenpo Gyatso (Mkhan po Rgya mtsho), 18, 133, 145, 147, 150
Khön ('Khon) family, 21, 124, 127, 131–32, 135, 137–38, 145, 153
Khön Könchok Gyalpo ('Khon Dkon mchog rgyal po, 1034–1102), 125
Khubilai Khan (1215–94), 137–38, 140
Khyenrab Chöjé Rinchen Chokdrup (Mkhyen rab Chos rje Rin chen mchog grub, 1436–97), 79, 111, 142, 152–53
Khyenrab Jampa Ngawang Lhundrup (Mkhyen rab byams pa Ngag dbang lhun grub, 1633–1703), 6, 18–19
Khyenrab Rinpoché (Mkhyen rab Rin po che). *See* Khyenrab Chöjé Rinchen Chokdrup
Khyentsé Wangchuk (Mkhyen brtse'i dbang phyug). *See* Jamyang Khyentsé Wangchuk
Khyungpo Naljor (Khyung po rnal 'byor), 145
Kodrakpa Sönam Gyaltsen (Ko brag pa Bsod nams rgyal mtshan, 1170–1249), 150
Kunga Drölchok, Jetsun (Rje btsun Kun dga' grol mchog, 1507–66), 14, 19, 136
Kunga Lekpai Jungné (Kun dga' legs pa'i 'byung gnas, 1704–60), 21
Kunga Sangyé (Kun dga' sangs rgyas), 151
Kunpang Doringpa / Kunsang Chökyi Nyima (Kun spangs Rdo ring pa / Kun bzang chos kyi nyi ma, 1449–1524), 1–3, 9, 13–17, 19, 27, 47, 59, 115, 121, 123–24, 126, 130–31, 135, 147, 152–53
Kunpang Tukjé Tsöndrü (Kun spangs Thugs rje brtson 'grus, 1243–1313), 127
Kunsang Pakpa (Kun bzang 'phags pa, 1389–1442), 148
Kushang Drakpa Gyaltsen (Sku zhang Grags pa rgyal mtshan), 141
Kyamodung (Skya mo dung), 71
Kyetsal Monastery (Skyed tshal), 4, 12–13, 111–13, 149, 152–53

L

Lama Dampa Sönam Gyaltsen (Bla ma dam pa Bsod nams rgyal mtshan, 1312–75), 138
Lama Nyamepa (Bla ma Mnyam med pa), 138
Lamdré / Path with the Result (Lam 'bras), 2, 9, 17, 19, 21, 124–27, 130–31, 133, 138–39, 154–55. *See also* Lobshé; Precious Teaching
Latö (La stod), 75, 140
Latö Lho (La stod Lho), 148
Lhachen Palbar (Lha chen dpal 'bar), 89, 146
Lhachok Sengé (Lha mchog seng ge, 1468–1535), 139
Lhakhang Chenmo (Lha khang chen mo), 132
Lhanyen Shambhar (Lha snyan Sham bhar), 105, 152
Lhasa Dzongpa (Lha sa Rdzong pa, d. 1544), 132, 148
Lhatong Lotsāwa (Lha mthong Lo tsā ba, b. 1512), 19
Lhundrup Tsé (Lhun grub rtse), 11, 87, 144,
Ling (Gling), 144

Lobshé / Explication for Disciples (Slob bshad), 3, 14, 16–17, 19, 124–25, 131, 153, 155. *See also* Lamdré
Lochen Jangchup Tsemo (Lo chen Byang chub rtse mo, 1303–80), 130
Lotön Dorjé Wangchuk (Lo ston Rdo rje dbang phyug), 140
Lowo Khenchen Sönam Lhundrup (Glo bo Mkhan chen Bsod nams lhun grub, 1456–1532), 135

M

Mahākāla, 9, 11, 17, 139, 144, 146, 151–52
Mahākaruṇika, 77, 141
Mahāmudrā, 128, 154
Mahāyāna, 115
Maitreya, 59, 63, 131, 133–34
Maitripa (1012–97), 113, 134, 141
Maksorma (Dmag zor ma), 9, 67, 136
Mangkar (Mang mkhar), 4, 7, 14–15, 27, 33, 124, 126
Mangtö Ludrup Gyatso (Mang thos klu sgrub rgya mtsho, 1523–96), 14, 134, 148
Mañjughoṣa, 29, 53, 61, 125
Māra, 20
Marpa Lotsāwa Chökyi Lodrö (Mar pa Lo tsā ba Chos kyi blo gros, 1012–97), 16, 113, 141
Menlung (Sman lung), 87–89, 143–44, 150
Menlung Guru (Man lung Gu ru, b. 1239), 150
Menlung Monastery (Man lung dgon pa), 103, 150
Merwin, W. S., 6
Mikyö Dorjé (Mi bskyod rdo rje, 1507–54), 13, 18, 20, 111–23, 136, 153–55
Milarepa, Jetsun (Rje btsun Mi la ras pa, 1040–1123), 113, 131, 154
Mipam Chökyi Wangchuk (Mi pham chos kyi dbang phyug, 1584–1630), 19–20
Moonlight of Elegant Explication (Darpa Sönam Lhundrup), 18
Mount Lalung (Bla lung ri bo), 13, 47, 129
Mount Samding (Bsam sdings kyi ri), 91
Mu (Rmu), 149
Müchen Könchok Gyaltsen (Mus chen Dkon mchog rgyal mtshan, 1388–1469), 153
Mudrapa Chenpo (Mudra pa chen po), 130
Mushong (Rmu gshong), 15, 124

N

Nairātmyā, 121, 155
Nakartsé (Sna dkar rtse), 136, 149
Nakgyal (Nags rgyal), 43, 127–29
Nakgyalma (Nags rgyal ma), 127
Nālendra Monastery (Nā lendra), 77, 125, 132, 135, 142, 148, 153–54
Namgyal Rabten (Rnam rgyal rab brtan). *See* Puntsok Rabten
Namgyal Sangpo (Rnam rgyal bzang po), 128
Namgyal Taktsé (Rnam rgyal stag rtse), 33, 126
Namkha (Nam mkha'), 139
Namkha Chökyong (Nam mkha' chos skyong, 1436–1507), 128, 130
Namkha Dorjé (Nam mkha' rdo rje, 1483–1550), 130–32, 146
Namkha Lhundrup (Nam mkha' lhun grub, d. ca. 1569), 148
Namkha Sangpo (Nam mkha' bzang po), 127
Namkha Tsewang Dorjé (Nam mkha' tshe dbang rdo rje, d. 1569), 148

Namsé Tongmön (Rnam sras mthong smon), 95, 103, 150
Nangchen Kunga Pak (Nang chen Kun dga' 'phags, 1357–1412), 147
Nāro Khecarī, 21, 58, 125, 134, 153. *See also* Khecarī; Vajrayoginī; Vārāhī
Nāropa (1016–1100), 16, 87, 113, 134, 141, 143–44
Necklace of Marvelous Gems (Jamyang Gawai Shenyen), 18
Nepal, 19
Nesar (Gnas gsar). *See* Tsi Nesar
Ngakchang Kunga Rinchen (Sngags 'chang Kun dga' rin chen, 1517–84), 9, 15, 20, 51–53, 132, 148
Ngari Gungtang (Mnga' ris Gung thang), 147
Ngawang Chögyal (Ngag dbang chos rgyal). *See* Drukpa Ngawang Chögyal
Ngawang Drakpa (Ngag dbang grags pa). *See* Dakchen Ngagi Wangchuk
Ngawang Namgyal (Ngag dbang rnam rgyal, b. 1494?), 13, 18, 136, 152–53
Ngor (Ngor). *See* Ngor Ewam Chöden
Ngor Ewam Chöden (Ngor E waṃ chos ldan), 9, 71–75, 138–39, 145, 153
Ngorchen Könchok Lhundrup (Ngor chen Dkon mchog lhun grub, 1497–1557), 138, 145
Ngorchen Kunga Sangpo (Ngor chen Kun dga' bzang po, 1382–1456), 138–39, 142, 153
Nigu (Ni gu) lineage, 89
Niguma (Ni gu ma), 145
Norbu Khyungtsé (Nor bu khyung rtse), 147
Norbu Sangpo (Nor bu bzang po, b. 1403), 152
Nubchen Sangyé Yeshé (Gnubs chen Sangs rgyas ye shes, b. 832), 151–52
Nyan Lotsāwa Darma Drak (Gnyan Lo tsā ba Dar ma grags), 138
Nyang (Nyang), 93, 103, 145–48, 150
Nyenyö Jashong (Mnyan yod bya gshong), 18
Nyingma (Rnying ma), 7–8, 11, 13–14, 20, 129, 146–47
Nyukla Dzong (Smyug la rdzong), 154

P

Padampa Sangyé (Pha Dam pa Sangs rgyas, d. 1105), 135
Padma Heruka, 129
Padmasambhava, Guru, 45, 127, 129, 146, 151
Pakmodru (Phag mo gru), 140
Pakmodrupa Dorjé Gyalpo (Phag mo gru pa Rdo rje rgyal po, 1110–70), 133, 154
Pakpa Lodrö Gyaltsen ('Phags pa Blo gros rgyal mtshan, 1235–80), 71, 137–38, 140
Pakpa Palsang ('Phags pa dpal bzang, 1318–70), 144, 147, 150
Pakpa Rinpoché ('Phags pa Rin po che). *See* Pakpa Lodrö Gyaltsen
Palkhor Dechen (Dpal 'khor bde chen), 95, 103, 148
Panam (Pa rnam), 11, 84, 87, 91, 124, 144–47
Pang Lotsāwa Lodrö Tenpa (Dpang Lo tsā ba Blo gros brtan pa, 1276–1342), 130
Pañjaranātha, 71, 139
Para (Spa ra), 29, 125
Path with the Result. *See* Lamdré
Pema Karpo (Padma dkar po, 1527–92), 149
Pema Wangchen Yangsang Tröpa (Padma dbang chen yang gsang khros pa), 42, 45, 95, 128–29, 135. *See also* Hayagrīva
Penkar ('Phan dkar), 55, 134

Penyul ('Phan yul), 134, 148
Porok Dodé Gönpo (Pho rog Mdo sde mgon po, 1195–1257), 103, 150
Potala, 150
Potrom protector chapel (Pho khrom mgon khang), 89
Precious Teaching (Gsung ngag rin po che), 3, 41, 115. *See also* Lamdré
Profound Path Temple (Lam zab lha khang), 71, 138
Puntsok Rabten (Phun tshogs rab brtan), 47–49, 130, 132
Putra, black, (Pu tra nag po), 105, 152

Q
Queen of Adepts (Grub pa'i rgyal mo), 47, 131

R
Rāhula (Gza' gdong), 45, 129
Rakta Yamāri, 125, 153
Ralung (Ra lung), 11, 95–97, 101, 148–49
Rangjung Rikpai Dorjé (Rang byung rig pa'i rdo rje, 1923–81), 155
Ratnabhadra / Könchok Sangpo (Ratna bha dra / Dkon mchog bzang po), 8, 13, 45–47, 128–29
Rechungpa Dorjé Drak (Ras chung pa Rdo rje grags, 1083–1161), 131, 154
Rikzin Gökyi Demtruchen (Rig 'dzin Rgod kyi ldem 'phru can, 1337–1407), 128–29
Rikzin Sangyé Tenpa (Rig 'dzin Sangs rgyas bstan pa), 128
Rikzin Tsewang Norbu (Rig 'dzin Tshe dbang nor bu, 1698–1755), 20
Rinchen Palsang (Rin chen dpal bzang). *See* Darpa Rinchen Palsang
Rinchen Sengé (Rin chen seng ge), 71, 139
Rinchen Tsöndrü (Rin chen brtson 'grus), 73, 140
Rinpung (Rin spungs), 9, 11–13, 111–13, 122, 136, 145, 152–53
Ripuk (Ri phug), 77–79, 83, 143
Rong (Rong), 11, 103, 151–52
Rongchen (Rong chen), 153
Rongchung (Rong chung), 97, 101, 149
Rongpa (Rong pa), 152
Rongpa Takshön (Rong pa'i Stag zhon), 103, 152. *See also* Takshön

S
Sachen Kunga Nyingpo (Sa chen Kun dga' snying po, 1092–1158), 125–27
Saktang Ding (Sag thang Ding), 41
Sakya (Sa skya), 2, 12, 53, 61, 73, 95, 113–15, 121, 124–25, 132, 135, 139–40, 148, 152
  masters, 19, 21, 49, 121, 124, 127, 131–32, 135, 137, 140, 142, 145, 153
  Para patron of, 29, 125
  Thirteen Golden Dharmas of (Gser chos bcu gsum), 2, 136
  tradition of Tibetan Buddhism, 2, 7, 9, 14, 17, 127, 130, 138–39
Sakya Lotsā (Sa skya Lo tsā). *See* Sakya Lotsāwa
Sakya Lotsāwa (Sa skya Lo tsā ba, 1485–1533), 61, 124, 132, 135
Sakya Paṇḍita Kunga Gyaltsen (Sa skya Paṇḍi ta Kun dga' rgyal mtshan, 1182–1251), 140
Śākyamuni. *See* Buddha Śākyamuni
Śākyaśrībhadra (1140s–1225?), 87, 134, 143–44

Salo Jamyang Kunga Sönam (Sa Lo 'Jam dbyangs kun dga' bsod nams). *See* Sakya Lotsāwa
Saltong Shogom (Gsal stong sho sgom), 154
Samantabhadra, 47, 129
Samding Dorjé Pakmo (Bsam sdings Rdo rje phag mo), 145, 149
Samding (Bsam sdings), in Yamdrok, 145, 149
Samding Monastery (Bsam sdings dgon pa), 89, 145
Sangkar Lotsāwa Pakpa Sherab (Zangs dkar Lo tsā ba 'Phags pa shes rab), 71, 137, 142
Sangpo Tashi, Panchen (Paṇ chen Bzang po bkra shis, 1410–78), 135–36
Sangyé Nyenpa (Sangs rgyas mnyan pa, 1505–69), 153
Sangyé Sengé (Sangs rgyas seng ge), 145–46
Sangyé Tönpa (Sangs rgyas ston pa), 145
Saraha, 141
Sarasvatī, 4, 6, 18
Sengé Tsé ruler (Sde srid Seng ge rtse pa), 131
Serkhang Monastery (Gser khang dgon pa), 77, 81, 139, 141, 143
Seryab (Gser g.yabs), 47
Shab (Shab), 61–63, 132
Shākya Chokden, Panchen (Paṇ chen Shākya mchog ldan, 1428–1507), 152
Shalu (Zha lu), 10–11, 15, 73–77, 81–85, 139–41, 143, 153
  crazy monks at, 81, 143
Shambhala, 20, 128, 150
Shambhar Monastery (Sham bhar gyi dgon pa), 11, 103, 151–52
Shang Gönpawa (Zhang dgon pa ba, 1053–1135), 41, 126
Shangpa (Shangs pa), 2, 7, 14, 145–46
Shangtön Chöbar (Zhang ston Chos 'bar). *See* Shang Gönpawa
Shangtsé Dadrak (Zhang rtse Zla grags), 129
Shar king (Shar rgyal po), 97, 149
Shara (Sha ra), 111
Sharchen (Shar chen). *See* Sharchen Yeshé Gyaltsen
Sharchen Yeshé Gyaltsen (Shar chen Ye shes rgyal mtshan, 1359–1406), 79, 142
Sharkhapa (Shar kha pa) family, 148–49
Sherab Sengé (Shes rab seng ge, 1251–1315), 151
Shigatsé (Gzhis ka rtse), 144
Shu Valley (Gzhu lung pa), 18, 111
Silnön Dorjé (Zil gnon rdo rje). *See* Silnönpa
Silnönpa (Zil gnon pa, b. 1493?), 9, 67, 136
Siṃhamukha, 154
Six Yogas, 154
Six-Branch Yoga, 41, 127–28, 130, 143. *See also* Kālacakra
Smṛti. *See* Smṛtijñānakīrti
Smṛtijñānakīrti, 87, 144
Sokdokpa Lodrö Gyaltsen (Sog zlog pa Blo gros rgyal mtshan, 1552–1624), 20
Sönam Lhundrup (Bsod nams lhun grub), 142
Sönam Pal (Bsod nams dpal). *See* Menlung Guru
Sönam Rabten (Bsod nams rab brtan), 89, 146
Sönam Rabten Palsangpo (Bsod nams rab brtan dpal bzang po). *See* Sönam Rabten
Spontaneous Unimpeded Intention (Rikzin Gökyi Demtruchen), 128–29
Śrīdevī, 136, 142
Stūpa that Liberates on Sight (Sku 'bum mthong grol chen mo), 41, 127

Sugati, 79, 142
Sugatigarbha. *See* Sugati
Swat Valley (Pakistan), 129

T

Ta En Kunga Rinchen (Ta dben Kun dga' rin chen, 1339–99), 137
Tai Situ Jangchup Gyaltsen (Ta'i Situ Byang chub rgyal mtshan, 1302–64), 140
Tak Pass (Stag la), 71
Ṭakkirāja, 136
Takshön (Stag zhon), 11, 87, 103–8, 144, 151–52
Taktsal (Stag tshal), 103, 150
Taktsang Lotsāwa (Stag tshang Lo tsā ba, b. 1405), 138
Taktsé (Stag rtse), 150
Tangtong Gyalpo (Thang stong rgyal po, 1361?–1485), 2
Tārā of Nyan (Gnyan sgrol), 71, 138
Tāranātha (Tā ra nā tha, 1575–1635), 143–44
Tarpa Lotsāwa Nyima Gyaltsen (Thar pa Lo tsā ba Nyi ma rgyal mtshan), 143
Tarpa Monastery (Thar pa dgon pa), 87–89, 143–44
Tashi Lhunpo Monastery (Bkra shis lhun po), 2, 9, 135–36
Tashi Paljor (Bkra shis dpal 'byor), 142
tea, 35–37, 79, 85, 142–43
Temple of the Path with the Result (Lam 'bras lha khang), 71, 139
Toghon Temür (r. 1333–68), 140
Treho Chökyi Gyatso (Tre ho Chos kyi rgya mtsho, d. 1547), 136, 152
Tri Namkha Sönam (Khri Nam mkha' bsod nams), 95, 147, 150
Tropu (Khro phu), 53–65, 133
  ḍākinī at, 53–59, 63–65
  Face-Viewing Temple (Zhal ras lha khang), 53, 59, 133
  great stūpa of, 9, 59, 134
Tropu Kagyü (Khro phu bka' brgyud), 133
Tropu Lotsāwa Jampai Pal (Khro phu Lo tsā ba Byams pa'i dpal, 1172–1236), 134
Tsang (Gtsang), 13, 71, 125–26, 132, 137, 140, 146, 153
Tsangnyön Heruka (Gtsang smyon He ru ka, 1452–1507), 128
Tsangpa Gyaré Yeshé Dorjé (Gtsang pa Rgya ras Ye shes rdo rje, 1161–1211), 148–49
Tsangpo River (Gtsang po), 11–12
Tsarchen Losal Gyatso (Tshar chen Blo gsal rgya mtsho, 1502–66)
  alias Carefree Vagabond (Yan pa blo bde), 27, 67
  ancestry, 140
  ascension to the throne of Butön, 15, 141
  birth, 27, 124
  and Bökharwa Maitri Döndrup Gyaltsen, 15, 152
  and Dakchen Ngagi Wangchuk, 3–4, 29, 125, 148
  death, 16
  and disease, 1, 11, 97–99, 149
  encounters with ḍākinīs and goddesses, 1–2, 9, 10–11, 14–15, 53–59, 63–65, 77, 133–35, 138, 140–41
  and Gorumpa Kunga Lekpa, 9, 13, 47–51, 130, 132
  and Karmapa Mikyö Dorjé, 13, 18, 111–23, 153
  and Khecarī, 2, 15, 53–65, 125, 134–35

and Kunga Drölchok, 13–14, 19
and Kunpang Doringpa, 1–4, 14–16, 19, 27, 47, 77, 115, 121–23, 126, 135
and Ngakchang Kunga Rinchen, 9, 15, 20–21, 51–53, 132
and the protector Takshön, 11, 87, 103–5, 144, 151–52
and Ratnabhadra, 8, 13, 45–47, 128, 149
Tsi Nesar (Rtsis Gnas gsar), 49, 89, 92, 130–32, 146
Tsongkha (Tsong kha), 73, 140
Tsongkhapa Losang Drakpa (Tsong kha pa Blo bzang grags pa, 1357–1419), 154
Tsurpu Monastery (Mtshur phu), 18, 154
Tupten Gepel Monastery (Thub bstan dge 'phel dgon pa), 4–5, 14, 33–35, 124, 126

U
Ü (Dbus), 3–4, 11–12, 29–31, 35, 125, 132, 135, 142, 148, 154
Uḍḍiyāna, 129
Üri (Dbu ri), 18
Utter Simplicity (Sprod med), 125

V
Vaiśravaṇa, 59, 79, 137
Vajrabhairava, 125
Vajradhara, 27, 47–49, 124, 130
Vajrapāṇi, 79, 142
Vajrapāṇi Nīlāmbaradhara. *See* Vajrapāṇi
Vajrāsanapāda, 135
Vajrāvalī, 125
Vajravārāhī. *See* Vārāhī
Vajrayāna, 2, 124, 126, 132, 141, 154
Vajrayoginī, 9, 14–15, 53–57, 124–25, 133–34, 149. *See also* Khecarī; Nāro Khecarī; Vārāhī
Vārāhī, 59, 133–34, 149. *See also* Khecarī; Nāro Khecarī; Vajrayoginī
Vasubandhu, 131
Virūpa, 130, 155

W
Wangden Tsé (Dbang ldan rtse), 147
Weapon to Open the Door to Speech (Smṛtijñānakīrti), 144
White Protector (Mgon dkar), 89, 146

Y
Yamdrok (Yar 'brog), 95, 100, 145, 149
Yamdrok Nakartsé (Yar 'brog Sna dkar rtse), 136
Yamdrok Taklung (Yar 'brog Stag lung), 136
Yüan dynasty, 137–38, 140

About Wisdom Publications

Wisdom Publications is dedicated to offering works relating to and inspired by Buddhist traditions. To learn more about us or to explore our other books, please visit our website at www.wisdompubs.org. You can subscribe to our e-newsletter or request our print catalog online, or by writing to:

Wisdom Publications
199 Elm Street
Somerville, Massachusetts 02144 USA

You can also contact us at 617-776-7416, or info@wisdompubs.org. Wisdom is a nonprofit, charitable 501(c)(3) organization and donations in support of our mission are tax deductible.

Wisdom Publications is affiliated with the Foundation for the Preservation of the Mahayana Tradition (FPMT).

TSARCHEN'S TIBET

Map continued from front endpaper